GoodFood
magazine

101 HOT & SPICY DISHES

Published by BBC Books
BBC Worldwide Limited
Woodlands
80 Wood Lane
London W12 0TT

First published 2004
Reprinted 2005 (four times), 2006
Copyright © BBC Worldwide 2004
All photographs © *BBC Good Food Magazine* 2004

All the recipes contained in this book first appeared in *BBC Good
Food Magazine*.

ISBN-13: 978 0 563 52115 0
ISBN-10: 0 563 52115 5

Edited by Sarah Miles

Commissioning Editor: Vivien Bowler
Project Editor: Sarah Emsley
Designer: Kathryn Gammon
Design Manager: Annette Peppis
Production Controller: Arlene Alexander

Set in Bookman Old Style, Helvetica and ITC Officina Sans
Printed and bound in Italy by LEGO SpA
Colour origination by Radstock Reproductions Ltd, Midsomer Norton

GoodFood magazine

101 HOT & SPICY DISHES
TRIED-AND-TESTED RECIPES

Editor-in-chief
Orlando Murrin

Contents

Introduction

Step into any supermarket anywhere in the country and you'll find a fantastic array of exciting and exotic foods and flavours from around the world. Gone are the days when home cooks took pride in turning out meals that were safe and predictable. Now every mealtime can be an adventure and, unless you want to, you never have to cook the same dish twice.

Of all the different cuisines now available to us, hot and spicy has become the most popular. These flavours seem to transport us to faraway destinations, and bring us sunshine in every mouthful. To help you on your way, we at *Good Food Magazine* have chosen over 100 of our favourite hot and spicy recipes and collected them together in this compact and comprehensive book.

All the recipes have been tested in the *Good Food* kitchen, guaranteeing you success every time. They're also well balanced and come with a nutritional breakdown so you can keep track of the calorie, fat and salt content.

Not only is every dish bursting with magical aromas and exciting flavours, the vast majority of them, including *Citrus and Ginger Turkey Steaks*, pictured opposite (see page 134 for recipe), can be made in under an hour and with the minimum of fuss. So, whether you're fixing yourself a spicy snack or cooking supper for six, mealtimes need never be boring or bland again.

Orlando Murrin

Editor, *BBC Good Food Magazine*

Conversion tables

NOTES ON THE RECIPES

• Eggs are medium in the UK and Australia (large in America) unless stated otherwise.

• Wash all fresh produce before preparation.

OVEN TEMPERATURES

Gas	°C	Fan °C	°F	Oven temp.
¼	110	90	225	Very cool
½	120	100	250	Very cool
1	140	120	275	Cool or slow
2	150	130	300	Cool or slow
3	160	140	325	Warm
4	180	160	350	Moderate
5	190	170	375	Moderately hot
6	200	180	400	Fairly hot
7	220	200	425	Hot
8	230	210	450	Very hot
9	240	220	475	Very hot

APPROXIMATE WEIGHT CONVERSIONS

• All the recipes in this book list both imperial and metric measurements. Conversions are approximate and have been rounded up or down. Follow one set of measurements only; do not mix the two.

• Cup measurements, which are used by cooks in Australia and America, have not been listed here as they vary from ingredient to ingredient. Please use kitchen scales to measure dry/solid ingredients.

SPOON MEASURES

• Spoon measurements are level unless otherwise specified.

• 1 teaspoon = 5ml

• 1 tablespoon = 15ml

• 1 Australian tablespoon = 20ml (cooks in Australia should measure 3 teaspoons where 1 tablespoon is specified in a recipe)

APPROXIMATE LIQUID CONVERSIONS

metric	imperial	AUS	US
50ml	2fl oz	¼ cup	¼ cup
125ml	4fl oz	½ cup	½ cup
175ml	6fl oz	¾ cup	¾ cup
225ml	8fl oz	1 cup	1 cup
300ml	10fl oz/½ pint	½ pint	1¼ cups
450ml	16fl oz	2 cups	2 cups/1 pint
600ml	20fl oz/1 pint	1 pint	2½ cups
1 litre	35fl oz/1¾ pints	1¾ pints	1 quart

If you can't get hold of a jar of Very Lazy Chillies,
just use chilli sauce or chilli paste instead.

Satay Shots

4 skinless boneless chicken breasts
3 tbsp soy sauce
1 heaped tbsp Very Lazy Chillies
2 garlic cloves, crushed
1 tbsp vegetable oil
1 heaped tbsp light muscovado sugar
415g jar ready-made satay sauce
1 lime, cut in half
12 lime slices

Takes 20–30 minutes • Makes 36

1 Cut the chicken breasts into 36 thin strips and put them into a bowl with the soy sauce, chilli, garlic, oil and sugar. Mix together until the chicken is coated, then thread each strip on to a bamboo skewer. Get the skewers lined up on a baking tray and keep covered in the fridge until ready to cook.

2 Preheat the oven to 190°C/Gas 5/fan oven 170°C. Put the tray in the hottest part of the oven for 10 minutes. Meanwhile, warm the satay sauce in a pan, then spoon into 12 shot glasses or small tumblers.

3 When the chicken is done, remove the tray from the oven and squeeze the lime juice over the chicken. Pop 3 skewers in each shot glass and a slice of lime on to each rim. Serve warm or cold.

• Per skewer 89 kcalories, protein 6g, carbohydrate 3g, fat 6g, saturated fat 1g, fibre 1g, added sugar 2g, salt 0.53g

Leftover cooked vegetables, with a curry kick,
make a warming and comforting soup.

Curried Vegetable Soup

1 tbsp sunflower oil
1 medium onion, chopped
2 celery sticks, chopped
2 medium potatoes, about 350g/12oz
total weight, peeled and cut into
small chunks
1 tbsp curry paste
1.2 litres/2 pints vegetable stock,
made from a stock cube
550g/1lb 4oz leftover roasted
or boiled vegetables, such as
Brussels sprouts, carrots, parsnips
and squash, roughly chopped
natural yogurt or crème fraîche,
to serve

Takes 30–45 minutes • Serves 4

1 Heat the oil in a large saucepan and fry the onion for 5 minutes until golden. Stir in the celery and fry for 5 minutes, then tip in the potatoes and fry for a further 1–2 minutes, stirring often.

2 Stir in the curry paste, let it cook for a minute or so, then pour in the stock. Bring to the boil and stir well. Lower the heat, cover and simmer for 15–20 minutes until the potatoes are tender.

3 Tip the leftover vegetables into the pan and warm through for a few minutes. Pour the soup into a food processor or blender and blitz to a smooth purée. Thin down to the desired consistency with hot water or stock (about 300ml/½ pint), then taste for seasoning. Serve in bowls with spoonfuls of yogurt or crème fraîche swirled on top.

• Per serving 211 kcalories, protein 8g, carbohydrate 21g, fat 11g, saturated fat 1g, fibre 7g, added sugar none, salt 1.19g

This quick and healthy supper is great for all the family.
Use chicken instead if you prefer.

Cajun Turkey Salad with Guacamole

2 tbsp sesame seeds
2 tbsp groundnut or sunflower oil
500g pack turkey breast steaks,
cut into strips
1 tbsp Cajun spice seasoning
1 large red pepper, seeded,
quartered and sliced
120g bag herb salad
130g tub guacamole
200g bag tortilla chips

Takes 20–30 minutes • Serves 4

1 Heat a large frying pan or wok, sprinkle in the sesame seeds and toss them over a fairly high heat for about a minute until they're slightly golden. Add the oil to the pan or wok, tip in the turkey, Cajun seasoning and red pepper and stir fry for about 5 minutes until the turkey turns from pink to white.
2 While the turkey's sizzling, divide the herb salad between four plates then, as soon as the turkey's done, spoon it over the salad, making sure to include all the spicy juices. Top each serving with a spoonful of guacamole, pile tortilla chips on the side of each plate and serve.

• Per serving 524 kcalories, protein 37g, carbohydrate 35g, fat 27g, saturated fat 5g, fibre 5g, added sugar none, salt 1.37g

A perfect family meal with only six ingredients. Teenagers will love making the wraps as they go along.

Mexican Chilli Wraps

500g pack lean minced beef
350g jar tomato and chilli sauce
8 large soft flour tortillas or
Mediterranean wraps
400g can red kidney beans,
drained and rinsed
142ml carton soured cream
100g bag herb salad

Takes 30–40 minutes • Serves 4

1 Dry fry the beef in a non-stick pan until it has changed colour all over. Spoon in a little of the sauce if the meat starts to stick. Add the rest of the sauce, then fill the jar about one-third full with water and rinse out into the pan. Bring to the boil, then let it bubble away for 15 minutes, stirring occasionally.
2 Dry fry the tortillas singly in a frying pan for 1 minute on each side. Meanwhile, add the beans to the meat. Stir well and heat through for about 5 minutes until the beans are hot and the meat sauce is thick.
3 Let everyone make their own wraps – spread the tortilla with some soured cream, then spoon the meat and some salad in the centre. Fold up one side of the tortilla, then fold in the sides to enclose the filling.

• Per serving 604 kcalories, protein 40g, carbohydrate 57g, fat 25g, saturated fat 10g, fibre 6g, added sugar none, salt 3.14g

These speedy canapés are best made to order, as they soften if allowed to stand around for too long.

Spicy Prawn Poppadums

24 cooked and peeled extra large tiger prawns, thawed if frozen
24 ready-to-eat mini poppadums, plain or assorted
200g tub tzatziki
a little chopped fresh coriander
paprika

Takes 10–15 minutes • Makes 24

1 Dry the prawns on kitchen paper and keep covered in the fridge. Lay out the poppadums on a serving platter. You can do this up to 2 hours ahead.
2 Just before serving, spoon a little tzatziki into each poppadum. Stand a prawn on top, then finish with a scattering of coriander and a light dusting of paprika.

• Per poppadum 58 kcalories, protein 5g, carbohydrate 4g, fat 2g, saturated fat none, fibre none, added sugar none, salt 0.92g

For a delicious sandwich filling for weekday lunches,
double the tuna mix.

Cheese and Paprika Tuna Melts

200g can tuna
½ bunch of spring onions,
finely chopped
4 tbsp mayonnaise
3 thick slices of granary or
wholemeal bread
50g/2oz cheddar, coarsely grated
1–2 pinches of paprika

Takes 10 minutes • Serves 2

1 Preheat the grill on its highest setting.
Drain the tuna, flake it into a bowl and mix
with the spring onions and mayonnaise.
Season with salt and plenty of freshly ground
black pepper.
2 Toast the bread under the grill until it's
nicely browned on both sides, then spread
the tuna mixture on top, right up to the
edges of the toast. Scatter over the cheese
and put back under the grill until the cheese
is bubbling.
3 Slice in half, sprinkle with paprika and
tuck in.

• Per serving (tuna in oil) 613 kcalories, protein 35g,
carbohydrate 29g, fat 40g, saturated fat 11g, added
sugar none, salt 2.25g

Just throw everything into a pan, leave it to simmer briefly
and – hey presto – your supper for one is ready.

Aromatic Soy Pork

150ml/¼ pint chicken stock
2 tbsp soy sauce
1 tbsp dry sherry
1 tsp Chinese five-spice powder
or 2 tsp five-spice paste
2.5cm/1in piece fresh root ginger,
peeled and finely sliced
1 garlic clove, finely sliced
½ bunch (about 4) spring onions,
trimmed and left whole
150–175g/5–6oz pork tenderloin,
sliced into long thin strips
about 50g/2oz flat rice noodles
a drizzle of sesame or vegetable oil
1 tsp toasted sesame seeds
1 small bok choi or a few Chinese
cabbage leaves, cut widthways
into 2.5cm/1in slices
handful of coriander leaves

Takes 35–45 minutes • Serves 1

1 Put the stock, soy sauce, sherry,
five-spice powder (or paste), ginger, garlic
and spring onions into a small saucepan
with a lid and bring to a gentle simmer.
After about 2 minutes, stir in the pork, cover
and let it simmer away, but not boil, for
about 5 minutes.
2 Put the noodles in a bowl with boiling water
and soak for 4 minutes. Drain the noodles
and toss with the oil and sesame seeds.
3 When the pork is ready, stir in the bok choi
or Chinese cabbage and simmer for 1 minute.
To serve, pile the noodles into a bowl, spoon
the pork and other bits on the top, pour the
broth around and scatter the coriander leaves
over. And don't forget to keep paper napkins
handy for those noodle slurps.

• Per serving 622 kcalories, protein 37g, carbohydrate
48g, fat 31g, saturated fat 10g, fibre 2g, added sugar
1g, salt 6.18g

Escabèche is a Chilean dish of Spanish origin that is usually based on lime juice or vinegar mixed with onions, peppers and spices.

Prawn and Avocado Escabèche

juice of 3 limes
5 spring onions, thinly sliced
1 tbsp tomato paste
1 large pinch of dried oregano
300g/10oz ripe tomatoes, cherry or plum, finely chopped
1 green chilli, seeded and finely chopped
400g bag large frozen cooked, peeled prawns
2 ripe avocados
3 tbsp chopped coriander

TO SERVE
iceberg lettuce leaves
ready-cooked poppadums

Takes 20–30 minutes • Serves 6–8

1 In a non-metallic bowl, mix the lime juice, spring onions, tomato paste, oregano, tomatoes and chilli. Season with salt and pepper, then cover with cling film. This mixture can now be kept in the fridge for up to 3 days.
2 Defrost the prawns and pat dry with kitchen paper. Just before serving, peel and cube the avocados. Add to the sauce with the prawns and coriander and mix well.
3 Carefully separate the lettuce leaves and arrange them over a serving platter. Spoon the prawns and juice into the cup-shaped leaves and serve with ready-cooked poppadums.

• Per serving 134 kcalories, protein 12g, carbohydrate 2g, fat 8g, saturated fat 1.5g, fibre 1.5g, added sugar none, salt 1.9g

If you prefer, you can cook the potatoes in the oven, unwrapped, at 200°C/Gas 6/fan oven 180°C for 1 hour.

Sticky Mustard Hot Dog Jackets

4 baking potatoes, each weighing about 225g/8oz
olive oil, for brushing
sea salt flakes
2 tbsp maple syrup or clear honey
1 tbsp balsamic vinegar
2 tsp wholegrain mustard
1 tsp tomato purée
8 pork sausages
leafy salad, to serve

FOR THE MUSTARD MAYONNAISE
8 tbsp mayonnaise
2 tsp wholegrain mustard
3 tbsp snipped chives or finely chopped spring onion

Takes about 1¼ hours • Serves 4

1 Rub the potatoes with a little oil, sea salt flakes and black pepper. Wrap each one in double-thickness foil and cook on the barbecue for 1 hour, turning frequently, until cooked.

2 Mix the maple syrup or honey, vinegar, mustard and tomato purée together to make a glaze. Brush over the sausages and cook on the barbecue, turning and basting often, for 10 minutes until cooked and sticky.

3 Meanwhile, mix the mustard mayonnaise ingredients in a small bowl.

4 Unwrap the potatoes and split them down the middle. Add the mustard mayonnaise and sausages (like a hot dog). Serve with a leafy salad.

• Per serving 740 kcalories, protein 19g, carbohydrate 56g, fat 50g, saturated fat 13g, fibre 4g, added sugar none, salt 3.94g

A classic snack for one,
with added spice.

Chilli Cheese Omelette

1 spring onion
a few sprigs of fresh coriander
2 large eggs
1 tbsp sunflower oil
½–1 tsp chopped fresh red chilli, or a
generous pinch dried chilli flakes
25g/1oz mild grated cheddar

Takes 10 minutes • Serves 1

1 Chop the spring onion and coriander quite finely and beat the eggs together with salt and pepper. Heat the oil in a small frying pan then tip in the onion, coriander and chilli and stir round the pan for a second or two so they soften a little. Pour in the eggs and keep them moving until two-thirds have scrambled.
2 Settle the eggs back down on the base of the pan, scatter over the cheese and cook for about a minute until the omelette is just set and the cheese has melted.
3 Carefully fold the omelette using a palette knife and slide from the pan to a serving plate. Eat while the omelette is hot and the cheese still melting.

• Per serving 381 kcalories, protein 22g, carbohydrate none, fat 33g, saturated fat 10g, fibre trace, added sugar none, salt 0.86g

Use small frozen peeled prawns rather than the bigger tiger prawns, so you get a good mix of ingredients on every forkful.

Prawn Salsa

2 large tomatoes
1 red pepper
198g can sweetcorn, or 175g/6oz
frozen, and thawed
2 tbsp chopped parsley or coriander
1 tsp Tabasco sauce
2 tbsp lime juice
2 tbsp light olive oil
300g/10oz cooked, peeled prawns,
thawed if frozen
2 ripe avocados
tortilla chips, to serve

Takes 10 minutes • Serves 6

1 Halve and seed the tomatoes and pepper. Chop the flesh into small pieces. Mix in a bowl with all the remaining ingredients, except the avocados. Cover with cling film and chill until ready to serve.

2 To finish the dish, peel, stone and chop the avocados and stir them in. Season to taste. Spoon into individual dishes and serve with a bowl of tortilla chips for everyone to dig into.

• Per serving 207 kcalories, protein 13g, carbohydrate 11g, fat 13g, saturated fat 2g, fibre 3g, added sugar 2g, salt 0.99g

These tasty home-made burgers use extra-lean mince lightened
with couscous and flavoured with herbs and chilli.

Leanburgers with Rocket and Peppers

50g/2oz couscous
500g/1lb 2oz extra-lean minced beef
1 small onion, finely chopped
2 tsp mixed dried herbs
3 tbsp chopped fresh chives
¼ tsp hot chilli powder
6 slices French bread
6 tsp Dijon mustard
175g/6oz roasted red peppers from
a jar, cut into large pieces
(choose ones in brine, or rinse
them if they're packed in oil)
a couple of handfuls of rocket

Takes 25–35 minutes • Serves 6

1 Tip the couscous into a medium bowl,
pour over 75ml/2½fl oz boiling water
and leave it for a few minutes to swell and
absorb all the water. Add the mince, onion,
dried herbs, chives and chilli powder, then
grind in plenty of salt and pepper. Mix
thoroughly, then shape into 6 oval burgers –
slightly larger than the bread slices. Cover
with foil and chill, for up to 24 hours, until
ready to cook.
2 Preheat the grill or barbecue, then cook
the burgers for 5–6 minutes on each side,
or more if you like them well cooked.
3 Grill and lightly toast the slices of bread
and spread with the mustard. Top with the
peppers, rocket and a burger and serve.

• Per serving 260 kcalories, protein 23g, carbohydrate
30g, fat 6g, saturated fat 2g, fibre 2g, added sugar
none, salt 1.1g

Add a touch of colour and spice to roasted potatoes
by parboiling them first with a touch of turmeric.

Golden Spiced Roast Potatoes

2.25kg/5lb floury potatoes,
preferably Desirée or King Edward
½ tsp turmeric
6 tbsp light olive or sunflower oil
½ tsp paprika
sea salt flakes

Takes 1 hour 40 minutes–1 hour
50 minutes • Serves 10

1 Preheat the oven to 190°C/Gas 5/fan oven 170°C. Peel the potatoes and cut into big chunks. Put them in a large saucepan of boiling salted water, sprinkle in the turmeric and give them a good stir. Bring back to the boil, then cover and simmer for 4 minutes.

2 Pour the oil into a roasting tin and put in the oven to heat through for 5 minutes. Drain the potatoes well in a colander and give a gentle shake to rough up the surfaces a bit.

3 Carefully tip the potatoes into the hot fat in the roasting tin, tossing with a big metal spoon to coat. Scatter with a light sprinkling of paprika and roast, without turning, for about 1¼ hours or until golden and crisp. Sprinkle the potatoes with sea salt flakes and freshly ground black pepper and serve immediately.

• Per serving 199 kcalories, protein 4g, carbohydrate 32g, fat 7g, saturated fat 1g, fibre 2g, added sugar none, salt 0.28g

As an alternative to Caesar salad dressing, mix 2 tbsp mayonnaise with ½ tsp Dijon mustard and a good squeeze of lemon juice.

Tuna Avocado with Spicy Dressing

200g can tuna in oil
1 large ripe avocado
2–3 tbsp Caesar salad dressing
1 tsp small capers
sprinkling of paprika or cayenne pepper
2 lemon wedges
2 handfuls of tortilla chips

Takes 10 minutes • Serves 2

1 Open the can of tuna and tip the contents into a sieve over a bowl. Leave for a few minutes so the oil drains off. Meanwhile, halve the avocado and remove the stone.
2 Season the avocado halves with salt and pepper, put them on two plates and spoon a little of the Caesar salad dressing into the cavities left by the stone. Flake the tuna on top, drizzle generously with the rest of the dressing and scatter with the capers and paprika or cayenne pepper. Serve with a wedge of lemon to squeeze over and a good handful of tortilla chips.

• Per serving 357 kcalories, protein 22g, carbohydrate 9g, fat 26g, saturated fat 2g, fibre 3g, added sugar none, salt 1.3g

Add some exotic mushrooms and a splash of white wine
or sherry to turn this simple snack into a treat for two.

Mustardy Mushroom Stroganoff

25g/1oz garlic butter, plus a little
extra for spreading
250g pack chestnut mushrooms,
thickly sliced
2 thick slices of granary bread
1 tsp wholegrain mustard
5 tbsp soured cream
a few fresh chives or spring
onion tops

Takes 10 minutes • Serves 2

1 Put a wok or frying pan over the heat.
Tip the butter into the pan and, when
sizzling, add the mushrooms and cook over
a high heat, stirring occasionally, until the
mushrooms are tender and juicy.
2 Meanwhile, toast and lightly butter the
bread. Put on 2 plates.
3 Stir the mustard and some salt and
pepper into the mushrooms with
4 tablespoons of the soured cream. When
lightly mixed, pile the mushrooms and their
creamy sauce on the toast. Spoon the
last of the soured cream on top, snip over
the chives or spring onion tops and grind
over some black pepper.

• Per serving 322 kcalories, protein 8g, carbohydrate
21g, fat 24g, saturated fat 14g, fibre 3g, added sugar
none, salt 1.08g

Sensational for a light meal, this easy-to-make broth
is packed with flavour and low in fat.

Teriyaki Chicken and Noodle Broth

1.4 litres/2½ pints hot
vegetable stock
1 tsp grated fresh root ginger
2 tbsp teriyaki marinade or light
soy sauce
½ tsp Chinese five-spice powder
85g/3oz fine egg or rice noodles
300g/10oz fresh stir-fry vegetables
85g/3oz mushrooms, halved
or sliced
100g/4oz skinless roast chicken,
torn into shreds
1 tsp sesame seeds
chilli sauce, to serve

Takes 15–20 minutes •
Serves 4, easily halved

1 Pour the stock into a large pan and heat
until just simmering. Stir in the ginger and
teriyaki marinade or soy sauce and then add
the five-spice powder.
2 Add your chosen noodles and cook
for 3–4 minutes, giving them a gentle stir
to loosen them up every now and then. Tip
in the stir-fry vegetables and mushrooms,
cook for a couple of minutes, then add the
cooked chicken and simmer for a further
1–2 minutes.
3 Season the soup to taste and serve it as
soon as possible. Ladle into four warmed
bowls and sprinkle with the sesame seeds.
Put the chilli sauce bottle on the table so
that everyone can fire up their soups with
more heat if they want to.

• Per serving (with egg noodles) 124 kcalories, protein
6g, carbohydrate 21g, fat 2g, saturated fat none, fibre
2g, added sugar none, salt 2.6g

Skinless chicken breasts, low-fat yogurt and a modest amount of
curry paste all help to keep this version of a classic dish low in fat.

Chicken Tikka Kebabs

150g carton low-fat natural yogurt
2 tbsp tikka masala curry paste
700g/1lb 9oz skinless, boneless
chicken breasts, cut into chunks
½ cucumber, chopped
2 large tomatoes, chopped
1 green chilli, seeded and finely
chopped
1 small onion, finely sliced
4 tbsp roughly chopped fresh
coriander
8 soft flour tortilla wraps or chapatis

Takes 1 hour • Serves 4

1 Mix the yogurt with the curry paste in
a large bowl. Add the chicken, season,
then stir really well. Cover and leave for
30 minutes at room temperature to give
the spices time to flavour the chicken.
2 To make the salad, mix together the
cucumber, tomatoes, chilli, onion and
coriander. Season lightly, then cover until
you're ready to serve with the meal.
3 Preheat the grill or barbecue. Push
the chicken on to 8 metal or wooden
skewers. Grill or barbecue the kebabs for
8–10 minutes, turning them frequently. At
the same time, warm the tortillas or chapatis
on one side of the barbecue, wrapping them
in foil. Serve two kebabs per person, with
two tortillas or chapatis and plenty of salad.

• Per serving 559 kcalories, protein 54g, carbohydrate
79g, fat 5.3g, saturated fat 1g, fibre 3.9g, added
sugar none, salt 1.53g

This fruity chutney is low in sugar with a spicy chilli kick – perfect with a big chunk of cheddar cheese and some freshly baked bread.

Sweet and Spicy Ploughman's

900g/2lb firm plums, stoned and
roughly chopped
1 onion, roughly chopped
5cm/2in piece of fresh root ginger,
grated or finely chopped
225ml/8fl oz orange juice
100ml/3½fl oz red wine vinegar
140g/5oz raisins
50g/2oz light muscovado sugar
1 cinnamon stick
½ tsp chilli flakes
25g/1oz blanched almonds, each
cut into 3 strips
cheddar cheese and fresh bread,
to serve

Takes 1–1¼ hours • Makes 900g/2lb

1 To make the chutney, put the plums, onion, ginger, orange juice, vinegar, raisins, sugar, cinnamon stick and chilli flakes into a large shallow pan. Bring to the boil and simmer for 30–40 minutes until the plums are tender, stirring occasionally at first, then more frequently in the later stages. The chutney is done when it has thickened but is still slightly liquid (it thickens further as it cools).
2 Stir in the almonds and boil for 5 minutes, stirring. Pour into warm sterilised jars and cool before sealing (it will keep for up to 3 months in the fridge).
3 When ready to serve, spoon some chutney on to a plate and serve with cheddar cheese and slices of fresh bread.

• Per 25g serving 33 kcalories, protein 0.4g, carbohydrate 7.1g, fat 0.5g, saturated fat none, fibre 0.6g, added sugar 1.4g, salt trace

This quick yet authentic Oriental soup is surprisingly
low in fat and very satisfying.

Chinese Chicken and Sweetcorn Soup

418g can creamed sweetcorn
1 chicken stock cube
2 generous pinches of Chinese
five-spice powder
pinch of chopped chillies (optional)
1 tbsp cornflour, blended with
1 tbsp cold water to make a
smooth paste
3 spring onions, trimmed and sliced
1 cooked chicken breast
(or 100g/4oz cooked chicken
from a roast), skin removed and
finely chopped
1 large egg, beaten
sesame oil (optional), to serve

Takes 10 minutes • Serves 2

1 Tip the sweetcorn into a large pan set over a medium heat. Pour in 500ml/18fl oz water, then crumble in the stock cube and sprinkle in the five-spice powder and chillies, if using. Mix everything together with a wooden spoon, then bring to the boil.
2 When the soup is boiling, stir in the cornflour mixture. Continue stirring until the soup thickens, then tip in three quarters of the spring onions, all of the chopped chicken and continue to cook over a highish heat.
3 When the soup returns to quite a rapid boil, turn off the heat and slowly drizzle in the beaten egg, stirring the soup all the time, so the egg sets in thin strands as you pour. Ladle into bowls and top with the remaining onion and drizzle with a little sesame oil, if you like.

• Per serving 428 kcalories, protein 24g, carbohydrate 70g, fat 8g, saturated fat 2g, fibre 2g, added sugar 15g, salt 5.45g

A new take on prawn cocktail with light and fresh flavours. Raw prawns give juicier, more flavoursome results than ready-cooked ones.

Spicy Prawn Cocktail

350g/12oz raw, peeled tiger prawns, thawed if frozen
1 clove garlic, peeled and finely chopped
1 red chilli, seeded and finely chopped
5 tbsp olive oil
2 vine tomatoes
1 tbsp lemon juice
1 tsp clear honey
1 tbsp chopped coriander
2 Little Gem lettuces
1 ripe avocado, peeled and stoned
handful of rocket leaves
Italian flatbread or toasted pittas, to serve

Takes 25–35 minutes, plus chilling • Serves 6

1 Pat the prawns dry with kitchen paper. Mix the garlic, chilli and prawns. Heat 1 tablespoon of the oil in a pan, add the prawns and stir fry for 2–3 minutes, until pink. Tip into a bowl and leave to cool, then chill for up to 8 hours.

2 Meanwhile, quarter the tomatoes and discard the seeds. Finely chop the flesh and tip into a bowl with the lemon juice, honey and remaining oil. Add the coriander, season and whisk until slightly thickened. Cover and chill for up to 8 hours.

3 Tear the Little Gem leaves into small pieces. Chop the avocado flesh. Fill six glasses with the lettuce, avocado and rocket leaves. Pile the prawns on top and spoon over the tomato and coriander dressing. Serve with Italian flatbread or toasted pittas.

• Per serving 176 kcalories, protein 10g, carbohydrate 2g, fat 14g, saturated fat 2g, fibre 1g, added sugar 1g, salt 0.25g

If you don't have any basil, add a dash of pesto to this simple
and superhealthy alternative to beans on toast.

Smoky Beans with Basil and Bacon

2 tbsp olive oil
1 small onion, finely chopped
2 rashers smoked back bacon
420g can of cannellini beans
2 large tomatoes, preferably
vine-ripened, roughly chopped
6 or so large fresh basil leaves
a few drops of Tabasco sauce
lightly toasted bread, to serve

Takes 10 minutes • Serves 2

1 Warm the oil in a medium saucepan.
Add the onion, stir well, then leave to cook
over a high heat for about 5 minutes, stirring
occasionally.
2 Meanwhile, snip the bacon in half
lengthways, then cook in a frying pan until
the fat is golden and crisp.
3 Open and drain the beans, then add
them to the pan with the tomatoes. Stir well
and cook for another few minutes until the
tomatoes have softened. Shred the basil and
add to the pan with salt, a generous grinding
of black pepper and a few drops of Tabasco
sauce. Spoon on to plates and top each
with the bacon. Serve with lightly toasted
bread on the side.

• Per serving 329 kcalories, protein 16g, carbohydrate
30g, fat 17g, saturated fat 3g, fibre 9g, added sugar
none, salt 1.42g

Dried mushrooms give the same deep taste as soy sauce but, as they are virtually salt free, they are much healthier.

Oriental Beef and Mushroom Soup

25g/1oz dried ceps or porcini
½ beef stock cube
1 tbsp sunflower oil
1 extra-lean sirloin steak,
about 140g/5oz
1 fresh red chilli, seeded and finely
chopped
2 garlic cloves, crushed
1 tsp finely grated fresh ginger
100g/4oz small broccoli florets,
halved
2 tbsp dry sherry
100g/4oz fine egg noodles
100g/4oz fresh beansprouts
25g/1oz watercress,
roughly chopped

Takes 20–30 minutes • Serves 2

1 Snip the mushrooms into a large measuring jug, pour over 1 litre/1¾ pints boiling water and crumble in the stock cube. Set aside.
2 Heat the oil in a large non-stick pan. Add the steak and cook over a high heat for 2 minutes on each side. Lift on to a plate.
3 Add the chilli, garlic and ginger to the pan with the broccoli and stir fry for about a minute. Spoon in the sherry and stir to remove any sediment from the pan. Pour in the stock and mushrooms and simmer for 4 minutes.
4 Pour a kettleful of boiling water over the noodles in a large bowl. Leave to soften. Add the beansprouts and watercress to the soup. Cook for 2 minutes. Drain the noodles, divide between two soup bowls, then ladle over the soup. Thinly slice the beef and pile on top.

• Per serving 488 kcalories, protein 30g, carbohydrate 48g, fat 15g, saturated fat 2g, fibre 2g, added sugar none, salt 2.26g

A colourful pork stir fry makes a healthy, tasty family supper that's ready in minutes.

Pork and Noodle Pan Fry

2 tbsp sunflower oil
300g bag small broccoli florets
half a 250g packet of thick egg noodles
450g/1lb lean pork, cut into strips
6 spring onions, chopped into 5cm/2in lengths
100g/4oz shiitake or chestnut mushrooms
180g jar Cantonese sweet and spicy stir-fry sauce
300g bag beansprouts
1 handful of roasted salted cashew nuts

Takes 10 minutes • Serves 4

1 Over a high heat, bring a pan of water to the boil. Heat the oil in a wok, tip in the broccoli and stir fry for 2 minutes until it starts to soften.

2 Tip the noodles into the boiling water and boil for 4 minutes until softened. Meanwhile, add the pork strips to the wok and fry until the meat changes colour. Add the spring onions and mushrooms and cook for a minute or so until the mushrooms start to soften.

3 Stir in the sauce until everything is well coated. Drain the noodles and toss into the wok with the beansprouts and cashews. Heat until the beansprouts start to soften slightly, then serve.

• Per serving 423 kcalories, protein 37g, carbohydrate 32g, fat 18g, saturated fat 2g, fibre 4g, added sugar none, salt 0.87g

This dish is just as good served cold the next day, mixed with a spoonful or two of mayonnaise, as a summer pasta salad.

Garlicky Tomato Pasta

8 small new potatoes, quartered, or a large baking potato peeled and cut into small chunks
200g/8oz pasta shells
4 medium tomatoes, the riper the better
3 tbsp good quality olive oil
1 fat clove of garlic, finely chopped or crushed
1 pinch of crushed chillies or chilli powder
grated cheese, to serve

Takes 20–30 minutes •
Serves 2 (easily doubled)

1 Fill a medium pan with boiling salted water and bring back to the boil over a highish heat. Tip the potatoes into the water and boil for 5 minutes. Tip the pasta into the same water, stir and continue to boil for about 10 minutes or until the pasta and potatoes feel soft when prodded with a fork.

2 Meanwhile, chop the tomatoes finely, as you would for salsa. Scrape the tomatoes and their juice off the board into a bowl. Season generously and mix in the olive oil, garlic and crushed chilli. Stir well.

3 When the pasta and potatoes are cooked, toss them in the bowl with the tomato sauce until evenly coated. Divide the pasta between two bowls and serve with a sprinkling of grated cheese.

• Per serving 617 kcalories, protein 16g, carbohydrate 102g, fat 19g, saturated fat 3g, fibre 6g, added sugar none, salt 0.1g

This rice dish is great with curry and will also give
an exotic edge to grilled meat or fish.

Spicy Indian Rice

2 onions, sliced
2 tbsp sunflower oil
1 heaped tsp salt
½ tsp turmeric
1 cinnamon stick
1 mugful of American long grain rice
(about 200g/8oz)
6 cardamom seeds, crushed
1 tsp cumin seeds
large handful of sultanas
large handful of roasted
cashew nuts

Takes 15–20 minutes • Serves 4

1 Fry the onions in the oil in a large frying pan for 10–12 minutes until golden.
2 Meanwhile, fill a large saucepan with water, bring to the boil and tip in the salt, turmeric and cinnamon stick. Pour in the rice, stir once and return to the boil, then turn the heat down a little so that the water is boiling steadily, not vigorously. Boil uncovered, without stirring, for 10 minutes, until tender but with a little bite. Drain the rice into a large sieve and rinse with a kettleful of boiling water. Leave to drain well.
3 Stir the crushed cardamom seeds into the onions with the cumin seeds and fry briefly. Toss in the sultanas and roasted cashew nuts, then the hot drained rice. Serve immediately.

• Per serving 317 kcalories, protein 5.6g, carbohydrate 55.7g, fat 9.5g, saturated fat 1.1g, fibre 1.2g, added sugar none, salt 0.77g

This light and elegant dish is ideal
for midweek entertaining.

Chilli Prawn Linguine

280g/10oz linguine pasta
200g/8oz sugar snap peas, trimmed
2 tbsp olive oil
2 large garlic cloves, finely chopped
1 large red chilli, seeded and finely
chopped
24 raw king prawns, peeled
12 cherry tomatoes, halved
handful of fresh basil leaves
mixed salad leaves and crusty white
bread, to serve

FOR THE LIME DRESSING
2 tbsp virtually fat-free fromage frais
grated zest and juice of 2 limes
2 tsp golden caster sugar

Takes 25–35 minutes •
Serves 6

1 Mix the dressing ingredients in a small bowl
and season with salt and pepper. Set aside.
2 Cook the pasta according to the packet
instructions. Add the sugar snap peas for
the last minute or so of cooking time.
3 Meanwhile, heat the oil in a wok or large
frying pan, toss in the garlic and chilli and
cook over a fairly gentle heat for about
30 seconds. Add the prawns and cook
over a high heat, stirring frequently, for
about 3 minutes until they turn pink. Add
the tomatoes and cook, stirring occasionally,
for 3 minutes until they start to soften. Drain
the pasta and sugar snaps well, then toss
into the prawn mixture. Tear in the basil
leaves, stir, and season with salt and pepper.
4 Serve with salad leaves drizzled with the
lime dressing, and warm crusty bread.

• Per serving 333 kcalories, protein 32g,
carbohydrate 42g, fat 5g, saturated fat 1g, fibre 3g,
added sugar 2g, salt 0.9g

Jazz up simple rice for a delicious
Chinese supper.

Oriental Egg-fried Rice

1 heaped tsp salt
1 mugful of American long grain rice
(about 200g/8oz)
1 cupful of frozen peas
2 tbsp sunflower oil
2 back bacon rashers, roughly
chopped
1 small red pepper, chopped
2 garlic cloves, thinly sliced
2 large eggs
1 heaped tsp Chinese five-spice
powder
spring onions, shredded, to serve

Takes 15–20 minutes • Serves 4

1 Fill a large saucepan with water, bring to
the boil and tip in the salt. Pour in the rice,
stir once and return to the boil, then turn the
heat down a little so that the water is boiling
steadily, not vigorously. Boil uncovered,
without stirring, for 8 minutes.
2 Throw in the peas and boil for a further 2
minutes, until the rice is tender but with
a little bite. Drain the rice and peas into a
large sieve.
3 Heat the oil in a wok and stir fry the bacon
for 3–4 minutes until crisp. Add the pepper
and garlic and stir fry for 2 minutes.
4 Beat the eggs, pour into the pan and stir
fry until the egg just sets. Toss in the Chinese
five-spice powder and the rice and peas. Top
with the shredded spring onions and serve.

• Per serving 350 kcalories, protein 12.7g,
carbohydrate 50.5g, fat 12.1g, saturated fat 2.6g,
fibre 3.2g, added sugar none, salt 1.37g

This simple, low-fat pasta recipe keeps pots and pans, and ingredients, to a minimum.

Spicy Tuna and Lemon Pasta

350g/12oz pasta shells
200g pack trimmed fine beans, cut into short lengths
200g can tuna in oil
grated zest of a lemon
1 heaped tbsp small capers
generous pinch of chilli flakes
olive oil, for drizzling

Takes 15–20 minutes • Serves 4

1 Cook the pasta in boiling salted water for 8 minutes. Add the beans and cook for a further 3 minutes until both the pasta and beans are just tender. Meanwhile, tip the tuna and its oil into a bowl and flake the fish, keeping the pieces quite large. Stir in the lemon zest, capers, chilli and plenty of salt and pepper.

2 Drain the pasta and beans, return them to the pan and toss with the tuna mixture. Add a little olive oil if you need to moisten everything. Serve the tuna and lemon pasta on its own or with a tomato and onion salad.

• Per serving 401 kcalories, protein 23g, carbohydrate 68g, fat 6g, saturated fat 1g, fibre 4g, added sugar none, salt 0.4g

Meatballs are great comfort food to satisfy all the family.
Look for them in supermarket chiller cabinets.

Mustardy Meatballs with Spaghetti

350g/12oz dried spaghetti
1 tbsp olive oil
350g pack Swedish meatballs
1 tbsp honey
2 tbsp wholegrain mustard
300ml/½ pint chicken or vegetable
stock (a cube is fine)
3 tbsp crème fraîche
4 spring onions, sliced

Takes 15–25 minutes • Serves 4

1 Cook the spaghetti according to the packet instructions. Meanwhile, heat the oil in a wide pan, add the meatballs and fry for 5 minutes, stirring, until browned all over.
2 Stir in the honey, mustard and stock. Bring to the boil, then reduce the heat and simmer for 5 minutes. Stir in the crème fraîche and spring onions and bring to a gentle simmer, just to heat through.
3 Drain the spaghetti, top with the meatballs and sauce, and serve.

• Per serving 628 kcalories, protein 26g, carbohydrate 75g, fat 27g, saturated fat 11g, fibre 5g, added sugar 3g, salt 1.93g

This Thai-inspired light and healthy salad is packed with fresh zingy flavours and is an absolute doddle to make.

Prawn Noodle Salad

200g/8oz green beans
125g (half a 250g pack) flat rice noodles
100g/4oz frozen sweetcorn
200g/8oz cooked, peeled prawns, thawed if frozen
½ bunch of spring onions, sliced diagonally
1 tbsp sweet chilli sauce, plus extra for serving
juice of 1 lime
1 tbsp fish sauce (*nam pla*)
handful of fresh coriander, roughly chopped

Takes 15–25 minutes • Serves 3–4

1 Cut the beans in half and cook them in a pan of boiling salted water for 3 minutes. Drain the beans into a sieve and cool under cold running water. Pat dry with kitchen paper.
2 Put the noodles and sweetcorn into a large bowl, cover with boiling water and leave for exactly 4 minutes. Drain and cool under cold running water. Shake as much water as you can from the noodles, then snip them into shorter lengths.
3 Tip the noodles and sweetcorn into a large bowl, add the beans, prawns and spring onions and mix well with your hands.
4 Stir together the chilli sauce, lime juice and fish sauce. Season lightly. Pour this over the salad and toss well. Scatter the coriander over and serve with extra chilli sauce.

• Per serving for four 144 kcalories, protein 14g, carbohydrate 20g, fat 1g, saturated fat none, fibre 2g, added sugar 1g, salt 1.69g

Use the empty tomato can as a nifty measuring jug to make this satisfying and healthy microwave meal even easier.

Quick and Easy Jambalaya

400g can chopped tomatoes with garlic
1 canful of easy-cook rice (see step 1)
1 red pepper, seeded and chopped
2 chorizo or other spicy sausages (such as kabanos), about 200g/8oz, skinned and chunkily chopped
2 handfuls of frozen sweetcorn kernels, or a 198g can, drained
1 large sprinkling of Cajun seasoning

TO SERVE
1 small handful of parsley, chopped (optional)
142ml tub soured cream

Takes 30–35 minutes • Serves 4 (generously)

1 Tip the tomatoes into a large microwave-proof bowl. Fill the empty can with rice and tip it into the bowl, then fill the can with water and pour it in. Stir in the pepper, chorizo, sweetcorn, Cajun seasoning and some salt and pepper to season.
2 Cover the bowl with cling film and pierce a couple of holes in it with a knife. Microwave the rice for 10 minutes on High. Tear off the cling film and stir well, then return the uncovered bowl to the microwave for another 12–15 minutes until the rice is done.
3 Take the bowl out of the microwave, cover it with a plate and leave to stand for 5 minutes before stirring in the parsley, if using. Serve the jambalaya straight from the bowl, with the soured cream to spoon over it.

• Per serving 537 kcalories, protein 18g, carbohydrate 87g, fat 16g, saturated fat 5g, fibre 2g, added sugar none, salt 0.94g

A tasty and superhealthy way of using up leftovers
from the Sunday roast.

Monday Night Rice

2 tbsp vegetable oil
1 egg, beaten with 2 tbsp water
1 onion, chopped
2 garlic cloves, crushed
1 heaped tbsp curry powder
2 tbsp tomato ketchup
85g/3oz frozen peas
250g/9oz cold cooked rice or
a 250g pack ready-cooked rice
175g/6oz cooked chicken or pork,
shredded into strips
a good splash of soy sauce

Takes 30 minutes • Serves 2–3

1 Heat half the oil in a large non-stick frying pan over a highish heat. Pour in the beaten egg and leave it to set for a minute. Flip it over and let it cook for a minute on the other side. Slide the omelette on to a board and set aside.
2 Heat the remaining oil in the pan and fry the onion until golden. Stir in the garlic, curry powder and ketchup. Add the peas and cook for 2 minutes. Add the rice to the pan with the shredded meat and 100ml/3½fl oz water. Cook over a medium heat for 6 minutes, stirring occasionally, until piping hot.
3 Meanwhile, roll up the omelette and slice it across into strips. Toss the omelette and soy sauce through the curried rice mixture. Serve with extra soy sauce.

• Per serving for three 349 kcalories, protein 25g, carbohydrate 35g, fat 13g, saturated fat 2g, fibre 4g, added sugar 2g, salt 0.84g

Lemon olive oil is a great addition to the storecupboard. Use it for dressings, sauces and for brushing over meat or fish before barbecuing.

Chilli, Crab and Lemon Spaghetti

350g/12oz spaghetti or linguine
1 garlic clove, peeled
½–1 fresh red chilli
20g pack flatleaf parsley
170g can crab meat
3 tbsp lemon olive oil
½ glass of white wine

Takes 15–20 minutes •
Serves 4

1 Bring a large pan of salted water to the boil, add the spaghetti and cook according to the packet instructions, stirring a couple of times to stop it sticking.

2 Finely chop the garlic. Halve, seed and finely chop the chilli. Roughly chop the parsley. Open the can of crab meat and tip the contents into a sieve. Drain well.

3 Heat 2 tablespoons of the oil in a large frying pan, add the garlic and chilli and fry for 1 minute. Tip the crab meat into the pan with the wine, season with salt and pepper and heat through for a minute or so, stirring.

4 Drain the pasta, return it to the pan and tip in the crab mixture, the last tablespoon of oil and the parsley. Toss everything together and serve.

• Per serving 401 kcalories, protein 14.2g, carbohydrate 65.3g, fat 10g, saturated fat 1.4g, fibre 2.8g, added sugar none, salt 0.27g

You won't need any accompaniments with this complete meal in a wok. Straight-to-wok noodles will save you time, too.

Spring Vegetable Noodles

2 tbsp olive oil
3 smoked back bacon rashers
100g/4oz fine asparagus, cut into bite-sized pieces
100g/4oz broccoli, cut into bite-sized pieces
2 garlic cloves, finely sliced
6 spring onions, trimmed, halved lengthways and quartered
½ tsp Chinese five-spice
150g pack straight-to-wok noodles
50g/2oz frozen petits pois
soy sauce, to serve

Takes 20–25 minutes • Serves 2

1 Heat the oil in a wok. Using scissors, snip the bacon into the hot oil and fry, stirring occasionally, for 2 minutes.
2 Tip the asparagus and broccoli into the wok with the garlic, spring onions and Chinese five-spice. Stir fry for about a minute, then top with the noodles and petits pois and drizzle over a tablespoon of water. Cover the pan and let everything steam for 4 minutes until the broccoli is just tender.
3 Mix everything together and serve straight away, with a bottle of soy sauce on the table so each person can add their own.

• Per serving 339 kcalories, protein 15g, carbohydrate 27g, fat 20g, saturated fat 4g, fibre 5g, added sugar none, salt 2.21g

To save time, boil half the water in a kettle
while the rest is boiling on the hob.

Spaghetti with Chilli, Lemon and Olives

500g fresh or dried spaghetti
5 tbsp olive oil
50g/2oz pine nuts
5 fat garlic cloves, peeled
good pinch of dried chilli flakes
2 lemons
handful of parsley, roughly
chopped
100g/4oz pitted green olives,
chopped if you like
5 tbsp grated fresh parmesan,
plus extra to serve

Takes 10 minutes • Serves 4

1 Put a large pan of water on to the boil for the pasta. Meanwhile, put the oil and nuts in a small pan and warm over a low heat. Crush the garlic into the pan and sprinkle in the chilli. Continue warming until the nuts are lightly toasted – make sure the garlic doesn't burn.
2 Grate the zest from both lemons, then cut one in half and squeeze out the juice. Once the pasta water is boiling, add a generous amount of salt and the spaghetti and cook according to the packet instructions.
3 Drain the spaghetti and tip into a serving bowl. Pour over the garlicky oil and toss well with the lemon zest and juice, parsley, olives and parmesan. Season well. Add more lemon juice to taste, and serve with extra parmesan.

• Per serving 573 kcalories, protein 19g, carbohydrate 59g, fat 31g, saturated fat 6g, fibre 5g, added sugar none, salt 1.7g

Straight-to-wok noodles come ready cooked in individual pouches so all you have to do is heat them up.

Asian Chicken in a Bag

4 boneless skinless chicken breast fillets, about 450g/1lb total weight
350g pack prepared stir-fry vegetables (from the chiller cabinet)
4 × 150g pouches straight-to-wok noodles (2 packs)
100ml sachet stir-fry sauce, such as black bean, sweet and sour or Thai soy sauce, to serve

Takes 30 minutes • Serves 4

1 Cut four large pieces of parchment paper, each about 35cm/14in square. Cut the chicken into strips.
2 Tip the vegetables, chicken, noodles and stir-fry sauce into a large bowl and mix well.
3 Pile a quarter of the mixture in the middle of each piece of parchment paper. Make a parcel by folding two sides of the paper into the centre and folding them together to seal, then folding and tucking under the cut paper edges. Repeat with the rest of the paper and ingredients, then put them in the fridge (you can do this the day before).
4 Microwave the parcels, one at a time, on High for 5–6 minutes. Serve with soy sauce for splashing over.

• Per serving 383 kcalories, protein 37g, carbohydrate 50g, fat 5g, saturated fat 1g, fibre 4g, added sugar 1g, salt 2.44g

Based on egg-fried rice, this straight-from-the-wok
supper is full of spicy flavour.

Spiced Rice with Prawns

200g/8oz long grain rice
175g/6oz frozen peas
2 tbsp vegetable oil,
plus a drop extra
1 onion, chopped
3 rashers streaky bacon, chopped
1 tbsp tikka masala curry paste
250g/9oz peeled, cooked tiger
prawns, thawed if frozen
1 egg, beaten
soy sauce, to serve

Takes 20–25 minutes • Serves 4

1 Tip the rice into a pan of boiling salted
water and simmer for 10 minutes, adding
the peas for the last 3 minutes. Drain well.
2 Meanwhile, heat the 2 tablespoons of oil
in a large frying pan or wok. Add the onion
and bacon and stir fry for 3–4 minutes,
until the onion starts to turn golden and
the bacon begins to cook. Stir in the curry
paste and cook for a few seconds, then tip
in the prawns and heat them through for a
minute or so.
3 Push the prawn mixture to one side of the
pan and add the drop of oil to the other side.
Pour the egg into the oil, stir until cooked like
scrambled eggs, then mix into the prawns.
Add the rice and peas and mix well. Serve
immediately, with soy sauce for sprinkling.

• Per serving 411 kcalories, protein 25g,
carbohydrate 50g, fat 14g, saturated fat 3g, fibre 3g,
added sugar none, salt 1.63g

A quick, tasty and filling pasta dish – just toss it together and serve.

Spaghetti with Hot Spanish Flavours

80g pack sliced chorizo sausage
good handful of flatleaf parsley
2 red peppers from a jar, in brine
or oil
300g/10oz fresh spaghetti
2 tbsp olive oil
50g/2oz finely grated fresh
parmesan, plus extra to serve

Takes 10 minutes • Serves 4

1 Put a pan of water on a high heat to boil. Meanwhile, snip the chorizo into strips with scissors, and chop the parsley and red peppers.

2 When the water is boiling briskly, add the spaghetti with a good measure of salt, stir and return to the boil. Cook for 3 minutes.

3 In a large frying pan, heat the oil, add the chorizo and peppers and plenty of black pepper. Cook for a minute or so, until heated through and the juices are stained red from the paprika in the chorizo. Scoop half a mugful of pasta water from the pan, drain the remainder and tip the spaghetti into the frying pan.

4 Add the parsley and parmesan, toss well and splash in the pasta water, to moisten. Hand round extra parmesan at the table.

• Per serving 444 kcalories, protein 18g, carbohydrate 46g, fat 22g, saturated fat 6g, fibre 3g, added sugar none, salt 2.21g

Try to find conserve with large pieces of fruit
in it for speedy Moroccan-style chicken.

Sweet and Spicy Apricot Chicken

1 tbsp olive oil
400g pack mini chicken breast fillets
1 tsp each ground cumin and
coriander
2 × 110g packs coriander and
lemon couscous
300ml/½ pint chicken stock (a cube
is fine)
2 tbsp chunky apricot conserve
100g/4oz frozen chopped
French beans
14 kalamata olives
small handful of fresh coriander

Takes 20 minutes • Serves 2
(generously)

1 Heat the oil in large non-stick frying pan.
Add the chicken pieces in a single layer
and sprinkle the cumin and coriander over.
Cook, without stirring, for 1 minute. Turn the
chicken over and cook for another minute.
2 Meanwhile, put the couscous in a
saucepan and pour over 400ml/14fl oz boiling
water. Bring back to the boil for 1 minute. Turn
off the heat, cover and soak for 5 minutes.
3 Meanwhile, add the stock to the chicken
with the apricot conserve, French beans and
olives. Season and simmer for 5 minutes.
4 Fluff the couscous with a fork and pile into
serving bowls. Spoon the chicken mixture
over and scatter with fresh coriander to serve.

• Per serving 514 kcalories, protein 56g, carbohydrate
38g, fat 16g, saturated fat 3g, fibre 3g, added sugar
8g, salt 5.24g

If you need an iron boost, try this hearty supper dish of slim strips of liver combined with crispy potatoes, bacon and spring onions.

Spicy Liver and Bacon Sauté

2 tbsp olive oil
400g/14oz cooked new potatoes, halved
4 spring onions, cut diagonally into 2–3 pieces
4 rashers unsmoked bacon, each snipped into four pieces
1 tbsp plain flour
1 tsp paprika, plus extra for sprinkling
175g/6oz lamb's liver, sliced into thin strips
1 small handful of flatleaf parsley, chopped
150ml/¼ pint hot vegetable stock (made with bouillon powder)
4 tbsp soured cream

Takes 20 minutes • Serves 2

1 Heat the oil in a frying pan. Add the potatoes and fry over a high heat until golden. Remove with a slotted spoon and set aside.
2 Add the spring onions and bacon to the pan and fry until golden. Meanwhile, mix the flour and paprika together, season and use to coat the strips of liver.
3 Add the liver to the pan and fry for 2–3 minutes. Return the potatoes to the pan with the chopped parsley and cook until hot. Divide the liver mixture between serving plates and keep warm.
4 Add the stock to the pan and boil rapidly. Stir to dissolve the pan juices and scrape all the crispy bits up from the bottom, then pour around the liver and potatoes. Serve topped with soured cream and an extra pinch of paprika.

• Per serving 570 kcalories, protein 32g, carbohydrate 41g, fat 32g, saturated fat 10g, fibre 3g, added sugar none, salt 2.5g

The stalks of pak choi are crisp and juicy when you bite into them, while the leaves are soft, with a faint mustardy flavour.

Hoisin Chicken with Cashews

1 red pepper, seeded and cut into chunks
2 skinless boneless chicken breasts, cut into the same size chunks as the pepper
1 small onion, very roughly chopped
5 tbsp hoisin sauce
2 heads pak choi, quartered lengthways
handful of salted cashew nuts
rice or noodles, to serve

Takes 20–25 minutes • Serves 2 (generously)

1 Tip all the ingredients, except the pak choi and cashew nuts, into a large bowl, add 3 tablespoons of water and stir until everything is evenly coated with sauce. Tip into a shallow microwave-proof dish, scraping out every last bit of sauce from the bowl.
2 Cover the dish with cling film and pierce it several times to release the steam. Microwave on High for 2 minutes.
3 Carefully peel away the cling film, add the pak choi and give everything a good stir. Cover with fresh cling film and pierce again, then return the dish to the microwave for a further 7 minutes. Uncover, watching out for the gust of steam, and stir in the cashew nuts. Serve straight from the dish, with rice or noodles.

• Per serving 334 kcalories, protein 39g, carbohydrate 25g, fat 9g, saturated fat 1g, fibre 3g, added sugar 12g, salt 1.76g

Mexican rice is a blend of cooked spicy rice and beans that just needs heating up. It's available from most major supermarkets.

Mexican Supper Pot

2 tbsp sunflower or vegetable oil
1 onion, chopped
450g/1lb minced pork or turkey
400g can chopped tomatoes
3 tbsp tomato purée
2 × 250g sachets ready-cooked Mexican rice
handful of fresh parsley, roughly chopped
plain tortilla chips, to serve

Takes 35–45 minutes •
Serves 4 (easily halved)

1 Heat the oil in a medium saucepan until hot, then tip in the onion and let it sizzle and turn golden (4–5 minutes) as you stir occasionally. Add the mince and cook until it's no longer pink, stirring to break it up and scraping the bottom of the pan so it doesn't stick. If it does, add an extra splash of oil.
2 Tip the tomatoes into the mince, then fill the can with water and pour this in. Add the tomato purée, give it all a good stir and let it come to the boil. Simmer, covered, for 25 minutes to cook the mince through.
3 Stir in the rice from both packets and let it heat through gently, then stir in the parsley. Serve with tortilla chips.

• Per serving 489 kcalories, protein 30g, carbohydrate 46g, fat 22g, saturated fat 5g, fibre 3g, added sugar 1g, salt 1.1g

If the weather is fine, cook this zesty chicken dish
on the barbecue instead of a griddle pan.

Sizzling Chicken Platter

4 boneless, skinless chicken
breasts, about 500g/1lb 2oz
total weight
1 tsp hot chilli paste or harissa
3 tbsp olive oil
1 tbsp lemon juice
1–2 lettuces, depending on size,
such as cos, batavia or Webb's
⅓ cucumber
½ bunch of radishes
25g/1oz pine nuts, toasted
handful of mint leaves

FOR THE DRESSING
2 ripe vine tomatoes, seeded
and diced
½–1 tsp hot chilli paste or harissa
1 tbsp lemon juice
4 tbsp olive oil

Takes 40–50 minutes • Serves 4

1 Lay the chicken in a shallow dish. Whisk
up the chilli paste or harissa, the oil, lemon
juice and a little salt in a small bowl. Pour over
the chicken and rub in to coat each piece.
2 To make the dressing, mix the tomatoes
in a bowl with the chilli paste, lemon juice,
oil and a little salt. Set aside.
3 Heat a griddle pan, then cook the chicken
for 6–8 minutes on each side until cooked
through. Remove and wrap in foil.
4 Spread the lettuce leaves over a serving
platter. Slice the cucumber and radishes and
scatter over the lettuce. Cut the chicken into
strips and toss with half the dressing in a
large bowl. Tip on to the salad and scatter
with the pine nuts and mint leaves. Drizzle
over the remaining dressing and serve warm.

• Per serving 377 kcalories, protein 32.2g,
carbohydrate 4g, fat 26g, saturated fat 3.7g, fibre
1.5g, added sugar none, salt 0.23g

Cooking for friends can be fuss-free with this simple
midweek one-pot lamb curry.

Spicy Lamb Curry

4cm/1½in piece fresh root ginger,
chopped
2 onions, quartered
6 garlic cloves
2 plump red chillies, seeds removed
1 large bunch of coriander
2 tbsp fennel seeds
2 tbsp ground coriander
2 tbsp ground cumin
1.6kg/3lb 8oz diced casserole lamb
2 tbsp olive oil
2 × 400g cans chopped tomatoes
2 tbsp tomato purée
300ml/½ pint lamb stock
200g/8oz frozen peas
handful of fresh mint

Takes 2¼ hours • Serves 8

1 Put the ginger, onions, garlic, red chillies
and two-thirds of the fresh coriander into a
food processor and whizz to a paste.
2 Toss the fennel seeds, ground coriander
and cumin with the lamb. Heat the oil in a
flameproof casserole and fry the lamb in
batches until browned all over. Return all the
meat to the pan, add the ginger paste and
cook for 8–10 minutes, stirring occasionally.
3 Stir in the chopped tomatoes, tomato
purée and stock. Bring to the boil, cover and
simmer very gently for 1½ hours until tender.
4 Stir in the peas, bring to the boil and cook
for 4 minutes. Season to taste. Chop the
remaining fresh coriander with the mint and
scatter over the curry. Serve with warm naan
breads.

• Per serving 481 kcalories, protein 43g, carbohydrate
12g, fat 29g, saturated fat 13g, fibre 3g, added sugar
none, salt 0.68g

Make a night in with friends a relaxed affair, by doing all the work before your guests arrive.

Hot Southern Chicken

6 skinless, boneless chicken breasts
450g/1lb small new potatoes
about 500g/1lb 2oz butternut squash
2 tbsp olive oil
25g/1oz butter
2 large onions, thinly sliced
2 plump red chillies, seeded and finely chopped
3 garlic cloves, crushed
2 tbsp plain flour
400g can chopped tomatoes
2 tbsp tomato purée
850ml/1½ pints vegetable stock
2 fresh corn cobs
175g/6oz cherry tomatoes
2 tbsp each chopped fresh mint and coriander, plus extra coriander to garnish
garlic ciabatta, to serve

Takes 1 hour 5 minutes–1 hour 20 minutes • Serves 6

1 Cut each chicken breast into 3 pieces. Halve any larger potatoes. Peel the butternut squash and cut into chunks. Heat the oil and butter in a large sauté pan and cook all the chicken in batches for 3–4 minutes until golden all over. Remove from the pan. Add the onions, chillies and garlic to the pan and cook for about 5 minutes. Sprinkle the flour over and stir well. Stir in the chopped tomatoes, tomato purée and stock. Return the chicken to the pan with the potatoes and squash. Bring to the boil, cover and simmer for 20 minutes.

2 Run a sharp knife down each corn cob to remove the kernels. Add them to the chicken with the cherry tomatoes. Simmer for 5 minutes. Stir in the herbs, season and garnish with the coriander.

• Per serving 383 kcalories, protein 42g, carbohydrate 34g, fat 10g, saturated fat 3g, fibre 4g, added sugar none, salt 1.24g

Combining liver with a colourful medley of vegetables makes a dish bursting with flavour and nutrients.

Liver and Red Pepper Stir Fry

1½ tbsp groundnut oil
225g/8oz lamb's liver, cut into strips
1 leek, diagonally sliced
1 red pepper, seeded and cut into rough squares
1 red chilli, seeded and finely chopped
1 tsp dried oregano
1 garlic clove, crushed
100g/4oz spring greens, thinly sliced
grated zest of an orange and 2 tbsp juice
2 tbsp medium dry sherry

Takes 25–35 minutes • Serves 2

1 Heat 1 tablespoon of the oil in a large non-stick frying pan. Add the liver and stir fry over a moderately high heat for 3 minutes until light brown – don't cook for longer or the liver will become rubbery. Remove to a plate, leaving the juices in the pan.

2 Tip the leek, red pepper and chilli into the pan with the rest of the oil and stir fry over a high heat for 2 minutes. Add the oregano, garlic and spring greens and stir fry for a further 30 seconds or so, until the greens have just wilted and turned a nice bright green.

3 Return the liver to the pan, then add the orange zest and juice and sherry. Season. Toss everything together on a high heat and serve immediately.

• Per serving 287 kcalories, protein 27g, carbohydrate 11g, fat 14g, saturated fat 3g, fibre 4g, added sugar none, salt 0.26g

This healthy casserole can be made in advance and frozen for easy midweek entertaining.

Spicy Spanish Chicken Casserole

3 tbsp olive oil
2 onions, sliced
8 skinless chicken thighs
1 tbsp plain flour, seasoned with a little salt and pepper
300ml/½ pint chicken stock
grated zest of 1 orange
juice of 2 oranges
150ml/¼ pint sherry
1 tbsp Worcestershire sauce
300g/10oz butter mushrooms, sliced
2 tbsp chopped fresh parsley
boiled rice, to serve

Takes 50 minutes–1 hour • Serves 4

1 Heat 2 tablespoons of the olive oil in a large heavy pan, then add the onions and fry for about 10 minutes until lightly browned and soft. Transfer to a plate.

2 Toss the chicken in the seasoned flour. Heat the remaining tablespoon of oil in the pan, add the chicken and fry evenly until browned. Pour in the stock, fried onions with their juices, the orange zest and juice, sherry and Worcestershire sauce. Bring to the boil, then reduce the heat, cover and simmer for 25 minutes.

3 Stir in the mushrooms and cook for 5 minutes. Taste and season with salt and freshly ground black pepper if necessary. Just before serving, sprinkle over the chopped parsley and serve with boiled rice.

• Per serving 375 kcalories, protein 41g, carbohydrate 14g, fat 14g, saturated fat 3g, fibre 2g, added sugar none, salt 0.82g

If you want a simple but special dish, try this unusual satay salad.
Only the chicken needs cooking – just barbecue, griddle or grill it.

Satay Chicken Salad

4 skinless, boneless chicken breasts
½ cucumber, halved lengthways
and sliced
1 small red onion, halved and
thinly sliced
140g/5oz beansprouts
handful of fresh coriander leaves
2 tbsp olive oil
1 tbsp lime juice

FOR THE DRESSING
5 tbsp crunchy peanut butter
3 tbsp lime juice
1–2 tbsp Thai red curry paste

Takes 30 minutes • Serves 4

1 Heat a griddle until hot. Season the chicken breasts and cook on the griddle for about 8 minutes on each side, until cooked through and seared in attractive stripes.
2 Meanwhile, toss the cucumber, onion, beansprouts, coriander, olive oil and lime juice together in a shallow salad bowl. Mix the dressing ingredients in a jug, using 1 tablespoon of the curry paste and a little water to give the consistency of single cream. Taste the dressing and whisk in another tablespoon of curry paste if you prefer more of a spicy heat.
3 Slice the griddled chicken diagonally and scatter over the salad. Drizzle some of the dressing over and serve the rest separately.

• Per serving 343 kcalories, protein 40g, carbohydrate 5g, fat 18g, saturated fat 1g, fibre 2g, added sugar none, salt 0.55g

This Italian version of shepherd's pie is a meal in itself
and makes clever use of ready-cooked polenta.

Spicy Polenta Pie

1 onion, chopped
1 tbsp vegetable oil
500g pack minced lamb or beef
420g jar tomato, mushroom and
red chilli gratinata or 400g jar
arrabiata sauce
500g ready-made polenta
50g/2oz parmesan, coarsely grated

Takes 45–50 minutes • Serves 3–4

1 Fry the onion in the oil for 5 minutes, stir in the mince and fry for a further 5 minutes until evenly coloured. Mix in the jar of sauce. Bring to the boil, then cover and simmer for 20 minutes, adding a splash of water if it starts to get too thick.

2 Preheat the grill to high. Cut the polenta into about 20 slices. Tip the mince into a shallow ovenproof dish (about 1.5 litre/2¾ pint capacity) and arrange the polenta on top in overlapping slices. Sprinkle with the cheese. Grill for about 5 minutes until the polenta and cheese are tinged brown at the edges.

• Per serving for four 457 kcalories, protein 32g, carbohydrate 28g, fat 25g, saturated fat 11g, fibre 4g, added sugar 3g, salt 2.98g

A delicious combination of sweet and spicy makes
a midweek supper that's full of flavour.

Cajun Chicken with Pineapple Rice

2 tbsp olive oil
1 red pepper, seeded and diced
200g/8oz frozen sweetcorn, or 340g
can sweetcorn drained
2 tbsp Cajun spice mix
250g/9oz long grain rice
1 chicken stock cube
4 skinless, boneless chicken breasts
227g can pineapple chunks in
natural juice

Takes 25–35 minutes • Serves 4

1 Heat 1 tablespoon of the oil in a heavy-based pan with a lid. Add the diced pepper, sweetcorn and ½ tablespoon of the spice mix and fry for a couple of minutes. Add the rice, pour in 700ml/1¼ pints water, then crumble in the stock cube. Bring to the boil and stir once, then lower the heat, cover and simmer very gently for 15 minutes until tender.
2 Meanwhile, rub the remaining spice mix into the chicken breasts. Heat the remaining oil in a large frying pan and fry the breasts over a medium heat for 6–8 minutes on each side until golden brown and cooked through.
3 Gently stir the pineapple and juice into the rice, then cook for a further 2–3 minutes. Taste for seasoning. Put the chicken breasts on top of the rice and serve.

• Per serving 524 kcalories, protein 40g, carbohydrate 71g, fat 11g, saturated fat 1g, fibre 2g, added sugar nono, salt 1 26g

Serve this colourful, hearty goulash in bowls,
topped with a dollop of low-fat yogurt.

Quickie Sausage Goulash

2 tbsp olive oil
454g packet low-fat sausages,
cut into big chunks
2 onions, roughly chopped
400g can chopped tomatoes
1 tbsp tomato purée
1 tbsp bouillon powder
1 tbsp paprika
good pinch of sugar
4 medium floury potatoes, cut into
large chunks
2 big handfuls of shredded
spring greens

Takes 40–50 minutes • Serves 4

1 Heat 1 tablespoon of the oil in a large saucepan and fry the sausage chunks until evenly browned. Remove and set aside.
2 Mix the remaining oil with the onions in the pan and cook over a high heat, stirring occasionally, for 5 minutes or until the onions are golden brown. Pour in the tomatoes, stirring in the bits from the bottom of the pan, then add the tomato purée. Fill the can up with water twice and pour into the pan. Sprinkle in the bouillon powder, paprika and sugar. Season well. Stir and bring to the boil.
3 Tip the potatoes into the pan, cover and simmer for 10 minutes, stirring occasionally.
4 Add the shredded greens and sausages and gently heat for 5 minutes, until the greens are tender. Taste for seasoning, then serve.

• Per serving 417 kcalories, protein 21g, carbohydrate 42g, fat 19g, saturated fat 5g, fibre 5g, added sugar 1g, salt 4.34g

You can buy hot or cold cooked chickens for this fresh and zesty salad at the deli counter in most large supermarkets.

Oriental Chicken and Peach Salad

2 × 1.5kg/3lb 5oz or 3 × 1kg/2lb 4oz
cooked chickens,
preferably free-range
4 large ripe peaches, stoned
200g/8oz mangetout, thinly shredded
lengthways
6 spring onions, very finely sliced
4 tbsp chopped fresh coriander
zest and juice of 2 limes
2 tbsp clear honey
2 tsp freshly grated root ginger
2 tbsp soy sauce
6 tbsp sunflower oil
1 tbsp toasted sesame oil
herbed couscous, to serve

Takes 25–35 minutes • Serves 8

1 Remove the meat from the chicken, cut into chunky strips and put in a large mixing bowl. Cut the peaches into wedges and reserve any juice. Add the peaches and juice to the chicken with the mangetout, spring onions and coriander.

2 Put the lime zest and juice, honey, ginger and soy sauce into a small bowl and season. Slowly whisk in the sunflower oil until it thickens, then whisk in the sesame oil. Toss with the salad and serve with herbed couscous.

• Per serving 520 kcalories, protein 49g, carbohydrate 9g, fat 32g, saturated fat 9g, fibre 2g, added sugar 3g, salt 1.05g

Curry paste adds an instant burst of spicy flavour
to this warming one-pot dish.

Hot Hallowe'en Beanpot

2 tbsp vegetable oil
1 onion, chopped
1 large potato, peeled and cut into
small chunks
500g pack lean minced lamb or beef
2 rounded tbsp curry paste
700g/1lb 9oz butternut squash,
pumpkin or swede, peeled and
cut into small chunks
415g can baked beans

Takes 45–55 minutes • Serves 4

1 Heat the oil in a large saucepan, add the
onion and cook over a fairly high heat for
5–8 minutes until it's really brown, giving it a
good stir every now and then so it doesn't
burn. Tip in the potato, stir for a minute, then
add the mince. Keep stirring to break up the
mince and cook until it's no longer pink.
2 Stir in the curry paste and cook for a
minute to fire up the spices. Stir in the
squash, pumpkin or swede and 300ml/
½ pint boiling water, then cover and simmer for
25–30 minutes, stirring occasionally, until the
vegetables and meat are tender and
everything is juicy. (You can now cool, chill and
freeze this, if you wish, for up to 2 months.)
3 Tip in the beans and stir well. Let them
heat through for a few minutes, then serve.

• Per serving 470 kcalories, protein 34g, carbohydrate
42g, fat 19g, saturated fat 6g, fibre 8g, added sugar
4g, salt 2.18g

The easiest curry ever! With no ingredients to be weighed, this dish is perfect for people on the go.

No-fry Thai Curry

2 rounded tbsp Thai green curry paste
400ml can coconut milk
2 skinless chicken breast fillets, very thinly sliced
1 red pepper, seeded and cut into chunks
3 spring onions, halved lengthways and cut into long pieces
1 cupful of frozen peas

TO SERVE
2 tbsp chopped fresh coriander or basil
rice or noodles

Takes 15–25 minutes • Serves 2

1 Stir the curry paste over the heat in a medium pan for a few seconds, then pour in the coconut milk and bring to the boil.
2 Add the chicken, red pepper, spring onions and peas, let it all start to bubble again, then turn down the heat and cook very gently for 5 minutes, until the chicken is tender but the vegetables still have some texture
3 Stir in the coriander or basil and serve spooned over rice or noodles.

• Per serving 579 kcalories, protein 41g, carbohydrate 15g, fat 40g, saturated fat 28g, fibre 3g, added sugar none, salt 1.75g

A hearty, healthy Moroccan stew is perfect for
sharing with family and friends.

Lamb with Apricots, Almonds and Mint

2 tbsp olive oil
550g/1lb 4oz lean lamb, cubed
1 onion, chopped
2 garlic cloves, crushed
700ml/1¼ pints lamb or
chicken stock
grated zest and juice of 1 orange
1 cinnamon stick
1 tsp clear honey
175g/6oz ready-to-eat dried apricots
3 tbsp chopped fresh mint
25g/1oz ground almonds
25g/1oz toasted flaked almonds
steamed broccoli and couscous,
to serve

Takes about 2 hours • Serves 4

1 Heat the oil in a large flameproof casserole. Add the lamb and cook over a medium-high heat for 3–4 minutes until evenly browned, stirring often. Remove the lamb to a plate, using a slotted spoon.
2 Add the onion and garlic to the casserole and cook gently for 5 minutes until softened. Return the lamb to the pot. Add the stock, orange zest and juice, cinnamon, honey and salt and pepper. Bring to the boil, then reduce the heat, cover and cook gently for 1 hour.
3 Add the apricots and two-thirds of the mint and cook for 30 minutes until the lamb is tender. Stir in the ground almonds to thicken the sauce. Serve with the remaining mint and toasted almonds scattered over the top.

• Per serving 439 kcalories, protein 33.8g, carbohydrate 22.3g, fat 24.4g, saturated fat 6.5g, fibre 4.2g, added sugar 1g, salt 0.84g

A speedy and flavoursome version
of a Jamaican favourite.

Jerk Pork with Rice and Beans

1 tbsp olive oil
3 tbsp Jamaican jerk sauce
4 small boneless pork loin steaks,
about 500g/1lb 2oz total weight
1 chicken stock cube
50g/2oz creamed coconut
(from a block)
1 bunch spring onions, trimmed
and sliced
2 x 250g packets vacuum-packed
ready-cooked basmati rice
410g can red kidney beans, drained

Takes 10 minutes • Serves 4
(easily halved)

1 Warm the oil in a large non-stick frying pan over a low heat while you tip the jerk sauce into a shallow dish and use to coat the pork steaks on both sides. Place them in the hot oil (reserve the sauce left in the bowl) and turn up the heat. Fry for 4 minutes on each side until the steaks are cooked and richly glazed.
2 Meanwhile, pour 150ml/¼ pint boiling water into a medium pan over a high heat and crumble in the stock cube and creamed coconut. Add the spring onions, stir, then tip in the rice and beans. Stir and heat gently, breaking down any clumps of rice. If the rice looks a little dry, add an extra splash of water.
3 Heat the reserved sauce in the frying pan with the pork. Pile the rice on to plates, top with the pork and spoon the pan juices over.

• Per serving 833 kcalories, protein 43g, carbohydrate 73g, fat 43g, saturated fat 19g, fibre 13g, added sugar 4g, salt 2.37g

This combination of great flavours makes a perfect speedy supper dish. Serve with rice or noodles or on its own for a low-fat meal.

Chicken and Mango Stir Fry

1 ripe mango
450g/1lb skinless, boneless chicken breasts
4 tbsp vegetable oil
1 bunch spring onions, trimmed and sliced diagonally
1 small nugget of root ginger, peeled and grated
1 garlic clove, crushed or finely chopped
350g bag fresh stir-fry vegetables
3 tbsp soy sauce
1 tbsp sweet chilli sauce

Takes 20–30 minutes • Serves 4

1 Cut the mango lengthways on either side of the stone, then peel off the skin and chop the flesh into cubes. Slice the chicken into thin strips.

2 Heat half the oil in a large frying pan or wok. Add the chicken and stir fry for 4–5 minutes until lightly coloured. Remove from the pan with a slotted spoon and transfer to a plate. Heat the remaining oil in the pan and add the spring onions, ginger and garlic. Stir fry for 30 seconds, then add the mango and vegetables and stir fry for a further minute.

3 Return the chicken to the pan and splash in the soy and chilli sauces. Stir until evenly mixed, then cover and cook for a further 2 minutes until the chicken is tender and the vegetables are slightly softened.

• Per serving 201 kcalories, protein 31g, carbohydrate 16g, fat 2g, saturated fat 1g, fibre 4g, added sugar none, salt 2.48g

Use cooked chicken for speed in this low-fat dish
that everyone will love.

Fruity Chicken and Coconut Curry

200g/8oz long grain, Thai or
basmati rice
1 tbsp sunflower oil
2 courgettes, cut into chunks
1 red pepper, seeded and cut
into chunks
375g/13oz skinless, boneless
cooked chicken, chopped into
chunks
1 bunch spring onions, finely
sliced diagonally
100ml/3½fl oz reduced fat
coconut milk
150ml/¼ pint chicken stock
1 tbsp Thai red curry paste
1 orange, segmented

Takes 25–30 minutes • Serves 4

1 Cook the rice in lightly salted boiling water
until just tender – about 12 minutes.
Meanwhile, heat the oil in a wok or large
frying pan. Add the courgettes and pepper.
Stir fry over a high heat for about 3 minutes
until just starting to brown. Add the chicken
and cook, stirring, for about 2 minutes.
2 Toss in the spring onions. Pour the
coconut milk, stock and curry paste over.
Heat until simmering, then cook, uncovered,
for 5–6 minutes.
3 Add the orange segments to the chicken
mixture. Heat for 1–2 minutes, then season.
Drain the rice and divide between four
warmed plates. Serve with the chicken.

• Per serving 445 kcalories, protein 30g, carbohydrate
58g, fat 11g, saturated fat 4g, fibre 2g, added sugar
none, salt 0.8g

You can chill and then freeze this dish once the vegetables and pork are cooked, for a tasty, time-saving supper.

Make-ahead Chinese Pork

4 carrots, peeled and sliced diagonally
600g/1lb 5oz pork fillet, cut into bite-sized pieces
1 large red pepper, seeded and chopped into large chunks
1 tbsp Chinese five-spice powder
2 tbsp soy sauce
1 chicken or vegetable stock cube, crumbled
1 bunch spring onions, white part left whole, green tops finely sliced
boiled rice or noodles, to serve

Takes 30–40 minutes • Serves 4

1 Toss all the ingredients, except for the sliced spring onion tops, together in a large pan. Cover the pan with a lid and chill until you're ready to eat.

2 Pour 600ml/1 pint boiling water over the pork and vegetables and give everything a good stir. Cover the pan and bring to the boil. Stir and cover again and simmer gently for 10 minutes until the vegetables are tender and the pork is cooked.

3 Just before serving, stir in the spring onion tops. Ladle into bowls with rice or noodles.

• Per serving 286 kcalories, protein 35g, carbohydrate 12g, fat 11g, saturated fat 4g, fibre 3g, added sugar none, salt 2.67g

The glaze is also great for pork or lamb chops, sausages and burgers. Try this with the Golden Spiced Roast Potatoes on page 34.

Sticky Fingers Chicken

2 tbsp Worcestershire sauce
2 tbsp orange juice
2 tbsp English mustard
2 tbsp clear honey
4 chicken thighs (skin on)
4 chicken drumsticks (skin on)

Takes 40–50 minutes • Serves 4

1 Spoon the Worcestershire sauce, orange juice, mustard and honey into a bowl and stir them together until they're evenly mixed, then brush all over the chicken pieces.
2 Lay the chicken pieces on the barbecue and cook for 30 minutes, turning and basting occasionally with the glaze from the bowl, until the skin has a wonderfully sticky glaze and the chicken is cooked through – the juices should run clear (not pink or red) when you prod near the bone with a fork. Alternatively, cook the chicken under a hot grill for 30 minutes, or roast in a preheated oven at 200°C/Gas 6/fan oven 180°C, for the same length of time.

• Per serving 220 kcalories, protein 31g, carbohydrate 9g, fat 7g, saturated fat 2g, fibre none, added sugar 8g, salt 0.4g

Couscous goes really well with lamb and a finishing touch
of chilli oil perks it up a treat.

Chilli Lamb with Couscous

2 tsp chilli paste or harissa
3 tbsp olive oil
2 lamb leg steaks
140g/5oz couscous
25g/1oz toasted flaked almonds
50g/2oz raisins
300ml/½ pint hot stock or water
chopped coriander or parsley
(optional), to serve

Takes 20–25 minutes • Serves 2

1 Whisk the chilli paste with the olive oil
and some salt and pepper. Drizzle about 1
tablespoon of the mix over the lamb and
rub on to coat both sides evenly.
2 Preheat the grill, then grill the lamb for
3–4 minutes on each side until well browned.
3 Meanwhile, tip the couscous, almonds
and raisins into a heatproof bowl. Pour over
the hot stock or water, cover with a plate
and leave for 5 minutes. Fluff up with a fork,
then fork in the remaining chilli oil. Pile the
couscous on two plates, top with the lamb,
and sprinkle with some chopped coriander
or parsley if you like.

• Per serving 609 kcalories, protein 51g, carbohydrate
54g, fat 22g, saturated fat 7g, fibre 2g, added sugar
none, salt 0.39g

Toast sesame seeds in a large heavy-based frying pan or wok, over a high heat, stirring for a few minutes until golden.

Stir-fried Beef with Hoisin Sauce

1 tbsp soy sauce
1 tbsp dry sherry
2 tsp sesame oil
1 fat garlic clove, crushed
1 tsp finely chopped fresh root ginger (or fresh ginger paste in a jar)
200g/8oz lean sirloin steak, thinly sliced across the grain
1 tbsp sunflower oil
1 large carrot, cut into matchsticks
100g/4oz mangetout, halved lengthways
140g/5oz mushrooms, sliced
3 tbsp hoisin sauce
1 tbsp toasted sesame seeds
Chinese noodles, to serve

Takes 20–25 minutes, plus marinating
• Serves 2

1 Mix together the soy sauce, sherry, sesame oil, garlic and ginger in a shallow dish. Add the steak and leave to marinate for about 20 minutes (or longer, if you have time).
2 When ready to cook, heat the sunflower oil in a large frying pan or wok until hot. Add the steak with the marinade and stir fry for 3–4 minutes over a high heat until lightly browned. Remove, using a slotted spoon, on to a plate, leaving the juices in the pan.
3 Toss the carrot in the pan and stir fry for a few minutes. Add the mangetout and cook for a further 2 minutes. Return the steak to the pan, add the mushrooms and stir well. Add the hoisin sauce and stir fry for a final minute. Sprinkle with the toasted sesame seeds and serve immediately with Chinese noodles.

• Per serving 390 kcalories, protein 33g, carbohydrate 20g, fat 9g, saturated fat 4g, fibre 6g, added sugar 8g, salt 2.41g

Look for quick-cook turkey steaks that have been flattened into thin escalopes – they make a great change from chicken.

Citrus and Ginger Turkey Steaks

2 tsp cornflour
4 quick-cook turkey breast steaks, about 300g/10oz total weight
1 tbsp sunflower oil
juice of 2 oranges
1 tsp grated fresh ginger
1 tsp clear honey
1 orange, peeled and cut into segments
1 pink grapefruit, peeled and cut into segments
1 tbsp fresh snipped chives or chopped parsley
rice and broccoli, to serve

Takes 30–40 minutes • Serves 2

1 Sprinkle 1 teaspoon of cornflour on to a plate, then press the turkey steaks into the cornflour to dust them lightly. Heat the oil in a large non-stick frying pan, until it is really hot. Add the turkey and fry for 3–4 minutes, turning once until golden on both sides – cook in batches if necessary. Transfer to a plate.
2 Add the orange juice, ginger and honey to the pan. Gently bring to the boil. Mix the remaining cornflour with 1 tablespoon of cold water and stir into the sauce. Stir on a gentle heat until thickened and syrupy. Season.
3 Return the turkey to the pan. Add the orange and grapefruit segments and heat through gently. Scatter over the chives or parsley and serve straight away with rice and broccoli.

• Per serving 310 kcalories, protein 39g, carbohydrate 25g, fat 7g, saturated fat 1g, fibre 3g, added sugar 2g, salt trace

A superhealthy, warm chicken salad gets a taste and texture boost with spicy flavours and creamy avocado.

Chicken Salsa Salad

2 tsp olive oil
1 tsp mild chilli powder
3 skinless chicken breast fillets,
total weight 350g/12oz, cut into
thick strips

FOR THE SALAD
300g/10oz white cabbage
generous handful of chopped,
fresh coriander
finely grated zest and juice of a lime
300g/10oz cherry tomatoes, halved
2 ripe avocados, stoned, peeled and
thickly sliced
410g can red kidney beans,
drained and rinsed
½ small onion or a whole shallot,
thinly sliced

Takes 30–40 minutes • Serves 4

1 Mix together the oil and chilli powder, then add the chicken and stir so that each piece is well coated in the spicy oil.
2 Finely shred the cabbage, preferably in a food processor. Tip into a large bowl and toss with the coriander and the lime zest and juice. Stir well, then add the tomatoes, avocados, red kidney beans and onion or shallot, and toss gently so you don't crush the ingredients.
3 Heat a large non-stick frying pan, add the chicken and stir fry for about 4 minutes until the pieces are cooked, but still juicy. Toss into the salad and serve while still hot.

• Per serving 352 kcalories, protein 30g, carbohydrate 20g, fat 17g, saturated fat 2g, fibre 9g, added sugar none, salt 0.87g

Don't be put off by the knobbly exterior of celeriac – underneath lies a creamy celery-flavoured flesh, the perfect partner for salmon.

Salmon with Mustardy Celeriac Mash

2 salmon fillets, about 100g/4oz each
4 tsp olive oil
700g/1lb 9oz celeriac, thickly peeled and cut into chunks
100g/4oz baby spinach leaves

FOR THE DRESSING
2 tsp wholegrain mustard
2 tsp lemon juice
1 pinch of sugar

Takes 25 minutes • Serves 2

1 Place the salmon fillets on a foil-lined grill pan. Brush with 1 teaspoon of oil and season.
2 Put the celeriac into a pan of cold, lightly salted water. Bring to the boil, then simmer for 12–15 minutes until tender. Preheat the grill to medium.
3 Grill the salmon for 5 minutes on each side. Meanwhile, drain the celeriac, leaving 1 tablespoon of water in the pan. Return the celeriac to the pan and mash over a low heat until fairly smooth. Add 1 tablespoon of the mustard dressing and the spinach and stir until wilted. Season to taste.
4 Divide the mash between two plates. Top with the salmon and the remaining dressing.

• Per serving 236 kcalories, protein 25g, carbohydrate 6g, fat 13g, saturated fat 2g, fibre 9g, added sugar none, salt 0.98g

Using mostly storecupboard ingredients, this dish is a meal in itself. Serve with crusty bread if you're hungry.

Dishy Fish Chowder

2 tbsp olive oil or sunflower oil
1 large potato, peeled and cut into big chunks
1 medium onion, chopped
1 fat garlic clove, finely chopped, or 1 tsp garlic paste
2 × 400g cans chopped tomatoes
2 tbsp tomato purée
½ tsp dried thyme
splash of soy sauce
410g can cannellini beans, drained and rinsed
500g/1lb 2oz plump white fish fillets, such as cod or hoki, in big chunks
handful of fresh parsley, chopped

Takes 20 minutes • Serves 4

1 Heat the oil in a large frying pan or wok. Dry the potatoes on kitchen paper and tip into the hot fat. Cook them, covered, over a medium to high heat for 5 minutes, stirring occasionally, until the potatoes are golden. Add the onion and garlic and cook for a further 3–4 minutes on a fairly high heat until the onion is nicely browned.

2 Stir in the tomatoes, the tomato purée, thyme and soy sauce, and let it bubble away for a couple of minutes. Stir in the beans and some salt and pepper, then sit the fish chunks on top, tucking them into the sauce. Don't stir or the fish will break up. Cover and simmer for 4 minutes, just until the fish is cooked. Serve sprinkled with parsley.

• Per serving 306 kcalories, protein 32g, carbohydrate 29g, fat 7g, saturated fat 1g, fibre 7g, added sugar none, salt 0.96g

For a low-fat version of this tangy and refreshing salad, use low-fat natural yogurt with a squeeze of lemon juice instead of mayonnaise.

Potato, Tuna and Horseradish Salad

750g/1lb 10oz baby new potatoes, halved
2 × 200g cans tuna in brine, drained
410g can haricot or butter beans, drained
2 celery sticks, thinly sliced
1 small red onion, finely sliced
25g pack fresh parsley, roughly chopped
2–3 tbsp creamed horseradish
4 tbsp mayonnaise
juice of 1 lemon
salad leaves, to serve

Takes 30–40 minutes • Serves 4

1 Put the potatoes in a saucepan of boiling salted water and cook for 10–15 minutes until tender. Drain well.
2 Tip the warm potatoes into a large serving bowl. Add the tuna, beans, celery, onion and parsley and mix thoroughly.
3 Put the horseradish, mayonnaise, lemon juice and 2–3 tablespoons of warm water into a small bowl and whisk well. Season lightly to taste. Drizzle over the salad ingredients and toss lightly. Serve on a bed of salad leaves.

• Per serving 388 kcalories, protein 27g, carbohydrate 42g, fat 14g, saturated fat 2g, fibre 6g, added sugar 1g, salt 1.79g

Spicy prawns and crispy baked potatoes are a quick
and easy Australian favourite.

Prawns with Tangy Mayonnaise

18 king prawns, uncooked and
in their shells
2 tbsp olive oil
baked potatoes and green salad,
to serve

FOR THE MAYONNAISE
200g jar of good-quality bottled
mayonnaise
2 limes
1 garlic clove, crushed
3 tbsp chopped fresh coriander

Takes 20–30 minutes • Serves 6

1 Tip the mayonnaise into a bowl. Finely
grate the zest of one of the limes into the
mayonnaise, then squeeze in the juice from
both, add the garlic and coriander, and stir.
Cover and chill.
2 Thread the prawns on to 6 skewers,
brush with the oil and put them on the
barbecue. Cook for 3–4 minutes on each
side until the shells turn pink and the flesh
inside looks white. Alternatively, cook the
skewered prawns under a preheated hot
grill for the same length of time. Remove
the prawns from the skewers and serve with
the mayonnaise, potatoes and green salad.

• Per serving 311 kcalories, protein 11g, carbohydrate
1g, fat 29g, saturated fat 5g, fibre none, added sugar
none, salt 0.67g

Make healthy and low-fat fish and chips a real treat
by serving them with a delicious orange raita.

Roast Spiced Fish and Chips

3 medium baking potatoes and
2 medium sweet potatoes,
each scrubbed and cut
lengthways into 6 or 8
wedges (no need to peel)
2 tbsp chilli oil or olive oil
4 white fish fillets, each weighing
about 175g/6oz
½ tsp cumin seeds

FOR THE ORANGE RAITA
1 large orange
¼ cucumber, finely chopped
1 small red onion, finely chopped
1 tbsp chopped fresh mint
1 tbsp white wine vinegar
3 tbsp low-fat natural yogurt

Takes 1 hour 10 minutes • Serves 4

1 Preheat the oven to 200°C/Gas 6/fan
oven 180°C. Tip the potatoes and sweet
potatoes into a roasting pan and drizzle with
the oil. Season, toss well, then roast for
40–45 minutes until tender, turning them
halfway through.
2 Meanwhile, peel the orange with a serrated
knife to remove the pith – do this over a bowl
to catch the juice, which you'll need later. Cut
out the segments, removing any membrane,
then chop them. Mix with the cucumber,
onion, mint, vinegar and yogurt. Add a little
salt and pepper, then set aside, covered.
3 Brush a baking sheet with oil and put the
fish on top. Season, sprinkle with the reserved
orange juice and the cumin seeds. Roast
above the chips for 12–15 minutes until the
chips are cooked. Serve with the orange raita.

• Per serving 318 kcalories, protein 36g, carbohydrate
29g, fat 7g, saturated fat 1g, fibre 3g, added sugar
none, salt 0.36g

Fresh tuna has a lovely meaty texture that's even better
when marinated before cooking.

Grilled Tuna with Spicy Bean Salad

2 fresh tuna steaks, about
175g/6oz each
1 tbsp olive oil
1 tbsp lemon juice
1 large garlic clove, crushed
1 tbsp chopped rosemary leaves

FOR THE SALAD
410g can cannellini beans,
drained and rinsed
8 cherry tomatoes, quartered
½ small red onion, thinly sliced
50g bag rocket
2 tbsp extra virgin olive oil
1 tbsp lemon juice
1 tsp wholegrain mustard
1 tsp clear honey

Takes 30–40 minutes, plus marinating
• Serves 2

1 Put the tuna in a shallow dish, drizzle over
the oil and lemon juice and scatter over the
garlic and rosemary. Turn the tuna so it's well
coated. Cover and put in the fridge for at
least 30 minutes.
2 Tip the beans into a large bowl. Toss in
the tomatoes, onion and rocket. Put the oil,
lemon juice, mustard, honey and some salt
and pepper in a screw top jar. Seal and set
aside.
3 Heat a cast iron ridged grill pan or frying
pan until very hot. Cook the tuna on a
moderately high heat for 2 minutes on each
side – don't overcook or it will be dry.
4 Shake the dressing. Pour over the salad
and mix together. Serve the salad with the
tuna on top.

• Per serving 565 kcalories, protein 54g, carbohydrate
30g, fat 26g, saturated fat 5g, fibre 9g, added sugar
2g, salt 0.67g

A super-quick microwave meal with only four ingredients and lots of flavour – what could be better for a midweek supper?

Creamy Cod in a Flash

2 skinless cod fillets, about
175g/6oz each
good handful of watercress leaves
(about ½ a bag)
4 rounded tbsp crème fraîche
1 rounded tbsp horseradish sauce
lemon wedges, to serve

Takes 10–15 minutes • Serves 2

1 Place the cod fillets side by side in a shallow microwave-proof dish and sprinkle with salt and pepper. Roughly chop the watercress and mix it in a bowl with the crème fraîche, horseradish and a little salt.
2 Spoon the sauce over each piece of fish (no need to spread it out). Cover with cling film, pierce it several times and microwave on High for 4–5 minutes (turning once if you don't have a turntable) until the fish is all white and starts to separate into flakes.
3 Take the dish out of the microwave and leave it to stand for 2–3 minutes with the cling film still on, then uncover and serve straight away, with lemon wedges for squeezing.

• Per serving 315 kcalories, protein 35g, carbohydrate 4g, fat 18g, saturated fat 8g, fibre 1g, added sugar 1g, salt 0.65g

Using canned chickpeas instead of potatoes means these
spicy patties are really quick to make.

Spicy Tuna and Chickpea Patties

150g tub low-fat natural yogurt
good handful of fresh coriander,
roughly chopped
2 × 410g cans chickpeas, drained
and rinsed
2 × 200g cans tuna in brine, drained
1 small onion, finely chopped
1 plump garlic clove, crushed
2 tbsp lemon juice
1 tsp cumin seeds
½ tsp crushed dried chillies
2 tbsp plain flour
4 tsp vegetable oil
12 cherry tomatoes, halved

Takes 25–35 minutes • Serves 4

1 Mix the yogurt with half the coriander in
a small bowl. Cover and chill.
2 Tip the chickpeas into a food processor.
Blitz for just a few seconds so they keep
some of their texture. Transfer to a large
bowl. Flake in the tuna and mix in the onion,
garlic, lemon juice, cumin seeds, dried
chillies and the rest of the coriander. Season,
then stir gently. Shape into 12 patties with
your hands. Dust with flour.
3 Heat half the oil in a large frying pan. Cook
6 patties for 5–6 minutes, turning them once.
Keep them warm while you cook the rest.
4 Put the tomatoes in the pan. Cook over
a high heat for 30–40 seconds until warmed
through and starting to soften. Serve with the
patties and the coriander dip.

• Per serving 327 kcalories, protein 33g, carbohydrate
32g, fat 8g, saturated fat 1g, fibre 6g, added sugar
none, salt 1.51g

This easy fish dish proves that reducing fat doesn't mean reducing flavour.

Haddock in Spicy Tomato Sauce

1 tbsp olive oil
1 onion, thinly sliced
1 small aubergine, about 250g/9oz, roughly chopped
½ tsp ground paprika
2 garlic cloves, crushed
400g can chopped tomatoes
1 tsp dark or light muscovado sugar
8 large basil leaves, plus a few extra for sprinkling
4 × 175g/6oz firm skinless white fish fillets, such as haddock
salad and crusty bread, to serve

Takes 40–50 minutes • Serves 4

1 Heat the olive oil in a large non-stick frying pan and stir fry the onion and aubergine. After about 4 minutes cover with a lid and let the vegetables steam fry in their own juices for 6 minutes – this helps them soften without needing to add any extra oil.
2 Stir in the paprika, garlic, tomatoes and sugar with ½ a teaspoon of salt and cook for another 8–10 minutes, stirring, until the onion and aubergine are tender.
3 Scatter in the basil leaves, then place the fish in the sauce, cover the pan and cook for 6–8 minutes, until the fish flakes when tested with a knife and the flesh is firm but still moist. Tear over the rest of the basil and serve with a salad and crusty bread.

• Per serving 212 kcalories, protein 36g, carbohydrate 8g, fat 4g, saturated fat 1g, fibre 3g, added sugar 1g, salt 0.5g

To make a warm salad, stir fry the prawns in the chilli dressing.
This fresh, tangy dish is also delicious with cooked chicken.

Spicy Prawn Salad

2 eggs
2 tbsp olive oil
3 tbsp lime juice, about 1 lime
2 tbsp sweet chilli dipping sauce
2 spring onions
1 Little Gem lettuce
198g can sweetcorn with peppers, drained
140g/5oz cherry tomatoes, halved
125g pack cooked, peeled tiger prawns

Takes 15–25 minutes • Serves 2

1 Bring a small pan of water to the boil. Gently lower in the eggs and boil for 8 minutes, then lift them out and plunge them into a bowl of cold water until you need them.
2 Whisk together the olive oil, lime juice and sweet chilli in a small bowl. Finely slice the spring onions on the diagonal, then mix them into the dressing.
3 Shell the eggs, and slice into rounds. Pull the lettuce apart and divide the leaves between two plates. Spoon the sweetcorn on top of the lettuce and scatter the tomato halves on top. Finish with the prawns and egg slices and douse everything with the chilli dressing.

• Per serving 383 kcalories, protein 25g, carbohydrate 28g, fat 20g, saturated fat 4g, fibre 3g, added sugar 7g, salt 4.32g

This easy main course, with its unusual flavours,
is smart enough for casual entertaining.

Sizzling Salmon with Bean Mash

4 skinless salmon fillets, about
175g/6oz each
1 lime
3 tbsp clear honey
1 tbsp wholegrain mustard
3 × 410g cans butter beans, rinsed
25g/1oz butter
5 tbsp crème fraîche
1 garlic clove, crushed
100g bag rocket

Takes 10 minutes • Serves 4

1 Set the grill to its highest setting. Put the salmon fillets skinned-side down and evenly spaced in a shallow flameproof dish. Finely grate the zest of the lime into a bowl, then squeeze in the juice and stir in the honey, mustard and a good sprinkling of salt. Pour the mixture over the salmon and grill, without turning, for 5–6 minutes until it's golden on top and cooked through (check the centre with a fork).

2 Meanwhile, tip the beans into a pan and add the butter, crème fraîche and garlic. Season well. Over a moderate heat, coarsely mash everything together until hot and bubbling. Add the rocket and stir into the mash until it's hot and just wilted.

3 Serve the salmon on the mash, drizzled with the cooking juices.

• Per serving 611 kcalories, protein 48g, carbohydrate 36g, fat 32g, saturated fat 11g, fibre 9g, added sugar 11g, salt 2.4g

A fishmonger is your best bet for large queen scallops; the small ones are available from supermarkets.

Scallops in Chilli Tomato Sauce

450g/1lb floury potatoes (such as King Edward), peeled and cut into chunks
3 tbsp olive oil
2 slices Parma ham
1 shallot, finely chopped
200ml/7fl oz fish stock (a cube is fine)
1 rounded tbsp sun-dried tomato and garlic paste
1 plump mild red chilli, seeded and finely chopped
8 large or 300g/10oz small queen scallops
3 tbsp finely chopped coriander

Takes 35 minutes • Serves 2

1 Cook the potatoes in lightly salted, boiling water for 12–15 minutes, until tender.
2 Meanwhile, heat 1 tablespoon of oil in a frying pan. Fry the Parma ham until crisp. Drain, tear into pieces and set aside. Fry the shallot in the same oil until softened.
3 Add 2 tablespoons of stock, the tomato and garlic paste and chilli to the pan. Cook for 1 minute. Add the remaining stock and boil until reduced by one-third.
4 Lower the heat, add the scallops and simmer gently for 3–5 minutes for small scallops, 5–6 minutes for large scallops.
5 Drain and mash the potatoes with the coriander and remaining oil. Season. Divide the mash between plates, spoon the scallops alongside and sprinkle with the crispy ham.

• Per serving 546 kcalories, protein 46g, carbohydrate 46g, fat 21g, saturated fat 4g, fibre 3g, added sugar 0.1g, salt 2.25g

An orange salad makes a refreshing contrast to the naturally oily texture of mackerel, while packing in the vitamin C at the same time.

Spiced Mackerel with Orange Salad

2 × 225g/8oz fresh mackerel, cleaned and heads removed (you can ask the fishmonger to do this for you)
½ tsp paprika
¼ tsp each ground cumin and coriander
1 tsp olive oil

FOR THE SALAD
3 small oranges
handful of flatleaf parsley, roughly chopped
1 small red onion, finely chopped
1 tsp extra virgin olive oil

Takes 25 minutes • Serves 2

1 Preheat the grill to high. Make three deep diagonal cuts into each side of each mackerel. Mix the spices into the oil and rub the mix all over the fish. Place the fish side by side in a shallow ovenproof dish.
2 Cook the fish under the grill for about 12 minutes, turning the mackerel over after 6 minutes, until cooked and nicely crisped.
3 Meanwhile, slice away all the peel and pith from the oranges using a serrated knife. Cut across the segments into rounds.
4 Add the parsley and red onion to the orange slices and toss together with the extra virgin olive oil. Serve with the spicy mackerel.

• Per serving 449 kcalories, protein 31g, carbohydrate 20g, fat 28g, saturated fat 5g, fibre 4g, added sugar none, salt 0.27g

Bags of frozen seafood are really handy – just use the amount you need and keep the rest for another time.

Chunky Chilli Seafood Stew

1 tbsp olive oil
1 small onion, chopped
1 garlic clove, crushed
1 pinch of fennel seeds or a
splash of Pernod, anisette
or Ricard (not
essential but does add flavour)
1 small pinch of chilli flakes
1 very small pinch of saffron strands
5 new potatoes, sliced
125ml/4fl oz white wine
220g can chopped tomatoes
¼ fish stock cube
200g/8oz frozen seafood cocktail,
defrosted
handful of chopped parsley
crusty bread, to serve

Takes 1 hour–1 hour 10 minutes •
Serves 1

1 Heat the olive oil in a medium saucepan and fry the onion on a low heat for about 7–10 minutes, stirring occasionally, until very soft and golden. Throw in the garlic, fennel seeds (if using), chilli flakes, saffron strands and the potatoes and continue to cook for a couple of minutes, stirring.
2 Pour the wine, and the Pernod (if using), into the saucepan and let it simmer for a couple of minutes. Stir in the tomatoes and two canfuls of water. Crumble in the quarter of stock cube, season, mix well, and simmer for 35 minutes, uncovered.
3 Stir in the seafood cocktail and simmer for 3–4 minutes until everything is piping hot. Scatter in the parsley, then serve straight away with some crusty bread to mop up the juices.

• Per serving 524 kcalories, protein 43g, carbohydrate 36g, fat 15g, saturated fat 2g, fibre 5g, added sugar none, salt 1.73g

This spiced yogurt is irresistible with salmon,
but would work well with lamb, too.

Spiced Salmon with Coriander Mash

1kg/2lb 4oz potatoes, peeled and
cut into chunks
2 tsp tikka or tandoori paste
200g tub Greek yogurt
4 salmon fillets
25g/1oz butter
½ tsp dried chilli flakes
large handful of fresh coriander,
chopped
4 tbsp or so milk
grilled tomatoes, to serve

Takes 25–35 minutes • Serves 4

1 Boil the potatoes for about 12 minutes until tender. Preheat the grill. Stir the spice paste into 4 tablespoons of the yogurt and smear the mixture all over the salmon. Put the salmon in a large flameproof dish, skin side up, and grill for 10 minutes.

2 Drain the potatoes and return to the pan. Add the remaining yogurt with the butter, chilli flakes, coriander and milk. Mash the ingredients together or use an electric hand whisk to beat the mash to a really creamy texture, adding extra milk if necessary. Pile on plates, top with the salmon and drizzle with the cooking juices. Serve with grilled tomatoes.

• Per serving 493 kcalories, protein 33g, carbohydrate 39g, fat 25g, saturated fat 9g, fibre 3g, added sugar none, salt 0.51g

You can get packets of special mixed frozen vegetables – petits pois, carrots, sweetcorn, green beans and red pepper – in supermarkets.

Speedy Veggie Biriyani

250g/9oz basmati rice
400g/14oz special mixed frozen vegetables
generous handful of raisins
1 vegetable stock cube
2 tbsp korma curry paste
generous handful of roasted salted cashew nuts

Takes 20 minutes • Serves 4

1 Pile the rice, frozen vegetables and raisins into a large microwave-proof bowl. Pour 600ml/1 pint boiling water over the rice mixture and crumble in the stock cube, then stir in the curry paste. Cover the bowl with cling film, leaving a small gap at the side to let out the steam. Cook in the microwave on High for 12 minutes.

2 Remove from the microwave and stand, still covered, for 5 minutes to complete the cooking – if you don't let it stand the rice will be too nutty. Fluff up the rice, scatter with cashews and serve.

• Per serving 305 kcalories, protein 9g, carbohydrate 57g, fat 6g, saturated fat none, fibre 2g, added sugar none, salt 1.42g

A simple dish, using mainly storecupboard ingredients, that's delicious served with a leafy green salad or peas.

Mustardy Cheese and Tomato Bake

225g bag baby leaf spinach
6 large eggs
425ml/¾ pint milk
1 tbsp English mustard powder
200g/8oz bread (about 3 thick slices)
200g/8oz mature vegetarian cheddar
4 clusters of cherry tomatoes on the vine

Takes 45 minutes–1 hour • Serves 4

1 Preheat the oven to 190°C/Gas 5/fan oven 170°C and butter a shallow 2 litre/ 3½ pint dish. Tip the spinach into a colander in the sink and pour a kettleful of boiling water over it. Leave it to wilt while you make the cheesy base.

2 Break the eggs into the bowl of a food processor, pour in the milk, add the mustard and 1 teaspoon of salt. Tear in the bread, crusts and all, then whizz together until smooth. Tip the mixture into a large bowl and grate in three-quarters of the cheese.

3 Squeeze the spinach to get rid of all the water, then stir it into the cheese mixture and tip into the dish. Grate over the remaining cheese, top with the tomato clusters and bake for 30–35 minutes until risen and golden. Cool and allow to settle a little before serving.

• Per serving 542 kcalories, protein 35g, carbohydrate 32g, fat 32g, saturated fat 15g, fibre 2g, added sugar none, salt 2.18g

Any curry leftovers will taste even better the next day.
This curry is also great with naan bread or chapattis.

Easy Lentil Curry

2 tbsp sunflower oil
2 medium onions, cut into rough
wedges
4 tbsp curry paste
850ml/1½ pints vegetable stock
750g stewpack frozen root
vegetables
100g/4oz red lentils
200g/8oz basmati rice
¼ tsp turmeric
handful of raisins and roughly
chopped parsley
poppadums and mango chutney,
to serve

Takes 40–50 minutes • Serves 4

1 Heat the oil in a large pan. Add the onions and cook over a high heat for about 8 minutes or until they are golden brown. Stir in the curry paste and cook for a minute. Slowly pour in a little of the stock so it sizzles, scraping any bits from the bottom of the pan. Gradually pour in the rest of the stock.
2 Stir in the frozen vegetables, cover and simmer for 5 minutes. Add the lentils and simmer for a further 15–20 minutes or until the vegetables and lentils are cooked.
3 Meanwhile, cook the rice according to the packet instructions, adding the turmeric to the cooking water. Drain well.
4 Season the curry with salt, toss in the handful of raisins and chopped parsley, then serve with the rice, poppadums and chutney.

• Per serving 432 kcalories, protein 14g, carbohydrate 76g, fat 10g, saturated fat 1g, fibre 6g, added sugar none, salt 1.38g

This fresh supper idea is fabulously low in fat. Once you've transferred it to the dish, it can be frozen for up to a month.

Curried Aubergine and Potato Pie

1kg/2lb 4oz potatoes, peeled and cut into 3cm/1¼in chunks
1 tbsp olive oil
1 large onion, chopped
2 large garlic cloves, crushed
2 large aubergines, cut into 3cm/1¼in chunks
1 tbsp medium curry powder
400g can chopped tomatoes
2 tbsp tomato purée
410g can green lentils, drained
green vegetables or salad, to serve

Takes 1 hour–1 hour 10 minutes
• Serves 4

1 Cook the potatoes in lightly salted, boiling water for 15–20 minutes until tender. Drain.
2 Meanwhile, heat the oil in a large frying pan and gently fry the onion and garlic until golden. Remove 2 tablespoons of the onion mixture and set aside. Preheat the oven to 220°C/Gas 7/fan oven 200°C.
3 Add the aubergines to the pan with the onions and cook gently for 6–8 minutes until softened. Add the curry powder and cook, stirring, for 1 minute. Add the tomatoes, tomato purée and lentils and cook for 2 minutes. Spread the mixture into a 2 litre/3½ pint dish and arrange the potatoes on top.
4 Scatter the fried reserved onions over and bake for about 35 minutes until browned. Serve with green vegetables or salad.

• Per serving 301 kcalories, protein 13g, carbohydrate 55g, fat 5g, saturated fat 1g, fibre 11g, added sugar none, salt 1.15g

The delicious flavours of this vegan salad make it the perfect dish for hot, sunny days. It's great on its own or as part of a summer buffet.

Spiced Butterbean and Tomato Salad

420g can butter beans, drained and rinsed
500g/1lb 2oz cherry tomatoes, quartered
2 small green or yellow courgettes (about 300g/10oz in total), chopped into small dice
1 small red onion, chopped
15–20g pack fresh coriander, chopped
2 tbsp lemon juice
3 tbsp olive oil
1 tsp ground cumin

Takes 15–20 minutes • Serves 6–8

1 Tip all the ingredients into a bowl with some salt and pepper and mix well. Cover and leave at room temperature until ready to serve. This salad can be made the day before and chilled.

2 Before serving, bring the salad to room temperature and give it a good stir.

• Per serving for six 109 kcalories, protein 4g, carbohydrate 9g, fat 6g, saturated fat 1g, fibre 3g, added sugar none, salt 0.41g

Potatoes take on spicy flavours beautifully and are especially good in a simple lentil and root vegetable curry.

Spicy Root and Lentil Casserole

2 tbsp sunflower or vegetable oil
1 onion, chopped
2 garlic cloves, crushed
700g/1lb 9oz potatoes, peeled and cut into chunks
4 carrots, thickly sliced
2 parsnips, thickly sliced
2 tbsp curry paste or powder
1 litre/1¾ pints vegetable stock
100g/4oz red lentils
1 small bunch of fresh coriander, roughly chopped
low-fat yogurt and naan bread, to serve

Takes 35–45 minutes • Serves 4

1 Heat the oil in a large pan and cook the onion and garlic over a medium heat for 3–4 minutes until softened, stirring occasionally. Tip in the potatoes, carrots and parsnips, turn up the heat and cook for 6–7 minutes, stirring, until the vegetables are golden.

2 Stir in the curry paste or powder, pour in the stock and then bring to the boil. Reduce the heat, add the lentils, cover and simmer for 15–20 minutes until the lentils and vegetables are tender and the sauce has thickened.

3 Stir in most of the coriander, season and heat for a minute or so. Top with the yogurt and the rest of the coriander. Serve with naan bread.

• Per serving 378 kcalories, protein 14g, carbohydrate 64g, fat 9g, saturated fat 1g, fibre 10g, added sugar none, salt 1.24g

Feta cheese and coriander add a fresh new twist to Mexican tacos, turning a quick meal into something special, oozing with flavour.

Feta Tacos with Guacamole

2 tbsp olive oil
2 medium red onions, cut into thin wedges
1 tsp cumin seeds
2 × 215g cans refried beans
10 cherry tomatoes
1 small pack fresh coriander
200g pack feta cheese
8 small flour tortillas
100g bag iceberg lettuce
2 × 130g tubs ready-made fresh guacamole
8 black olives, optional

Takes 10 minutes • Serves 4

1 Preheat the oven to 190°C/Gas 5/fan oven 170°C. Heat the oil in a large frying pan, add the onions and cumin seeds and fry until softened.
2 Tip the beans into the pan with the onions and start to warm. Halve the tomatoes, chop the coriander and dice the feta. Add to the pan and heat gently until just bubbling.
3 Place the tortillas directly on the oven shelves and heat for 1–2 minutes until warm and starting to puff. Now get everyone to help themselves and create their own tacos. Pile pieces of lettuce on the warmed tortillas and add a spoonful of the spicy bean and feta mixture. Top with a spoonful of guacamole, and an olive if you like. Fold over and eat with your fingers.

• Per serving 528 kcalories, protein 21g, carbohydrate 56g, fat 26g, saturated fat 8g, fibre 4g, added sugar none, salt 3.6g

You can use any mix of seasonal vegetables in this spicy Moroccan tagine, provided they will all cook in a similar time.

Vegetable and Chickpea Tagine

3 tbsp olive oil
1 large onion, chopped
2 garlic cloves, crushed
2.5cm/1in piece fresh ginger, grated
2 good pinches of saffron strands
2 tsp cumin seeds
1 cinnamon stick
1–2 tsp harissa
2 medium potatoes and 2 parsnips, peeled and cut into chunks
3 medium carrots, peeled and cut into chunks
4 celery sticks, sliced
2 medium leeks, sliced
400g can chopped tomatoes
600ml/1 pint vegetable stock
400g can chickpeas, drained
cooked couscous and fresh mint leaves or chopped parsley, to serve

Takes 1½–1¾ hours • Serves 4

1 Heat the oil in a large pan and fry the onion, garlic and ginger for about 5 minutes until soft. Crush the saffron and cumin seeds using a pestle and mortar, tip into the pan and fry for a further minute. Add the cinnamon stick and harissa. Season.
2 Add the vegetables and stir to coat them in the spicy mixture. Stir in the tomatoes, their juice and the vegetable stock, bring to the boil, then turn down the heat, cover and cook for 50 minutes–1 hour.
3 Once the vegetables are tender, add the chickpeas, seasoning to taste, and cook for a few more minutes to heat through. Serve with couscous and scatter with the mint or parsley.

• Per serving 305 kcalories, protein 11g, carbohydrate 40g, fat 12g, saturated fat 1g, fibre 10g, added sugar none, salt 1.2g

This easy pizza offers something different for vegetarians. Try to find a pizza base with a doughy texture and a crusty underside.

Spicy Florentine Pizza

30cm/12in bought pizza base
6 rounded tbsp bought tomato and chilli sauce
175g/6oz washed spinach leaves
about a third of a 290g jar antipasti mushrooms
50g/2oz parmesan, finely grated
4 medium eggs

Takes 30 minutes • Serves 4

1 Preheat the oven to 200°C/Gas 6/fan oven 180°C. Put the pizza base on a baking sheet and spread with the sauce.
2 Cook the spinach in a covered pan for 2–3 minutes. Drain and spread the spinach over the pizza base, then get the mushrooms out of the jar with a fork and scatter them over the top. Season and sprinkle with half the parmesan. Bake for 10 minutes.
3 Make four dips in the spinach with the back of a spoon, and crack an egg into each. Sprinkle with the remaining cheese and bake for a further 6–8 minutes, until the eggs are just set.

• Per serving 265 kcalories, protein 15g, carbohydrate 22g, fat 13g, saturated fat 5g, fibre 2g, added sugar none, salt 1.62g

This soup-stew is full of fragrant flavours. Try to find vegetable bouillon powder, which will give a more subtle effect than a stock cube.

Exotic Squash and Butterbean Stew

2 tbsp vegetable oil
1 large onion, chopped
1 butternut squash, about 900g/2lb
2 tsp muscovado sugar
400ml can coconut milk
225ml/8fl oz vegetable stock
2 pinches of dried crushed chillies
410g can butterbeans, drained and rinsed
finely grated zest of 1 lime
good handful of fresh coriander

TO SERVE
100g/4oz Thai or basmati rice, cooked
a few salted roasted cashew nuts, roughly broken or chopped

Takes 35–45 minutes • Serves 4

1 Heat the oil in a large frying pan and fry the onion until golden. Meanwhile, quarter the squash and discard the seeds. Cut away the hard outer skin and chop the flesh into chunks. Add to the pan with the sugar and fry for a few minutes until slightly caramelised.

2 Add the coconut milk, stock and dried chillies. Simmer gently, uncovered, for 20 minutes until the squash is tender.

3 Add the butterbeans and cook until heated through. Stir in the lime zest and coriander and season to taste with a little salt.

4 Put a spoonful of cooked rice into each soup bowl and ladle the soup-stew over. Scatter the cashews over and serve.

• Per serving 363 kcalories, protein 8g, carbohydrate 35g, fat 22g, saturated fat 15g, fibre 7g, added sugar 3g, salt 1.13g

Adding dried fruit, fresh mint and warm spices to savoury dishes is typical of North-African cooking.

Spiced Veggie Mince with Couscous

2 tbsp sunflower oil
2 medium onions, roughly chopped
350g pack Quorn mince
1 tbsp ground cumin
1 tsp cinnamon
2 tsp ground turmeric
100g/4oz ready-to-eat dried apricots, quartered
600ml/1 pint vegetable stock
50g/2oz unsalted cashews, toasted under the grill

FOR THE COUSCOUS
280g/10oz couscous
grated zest of 2 lemons
4 tbsp chopped fresh mint

Takes 35–40 minutes • Serves 4

1 Heat the oil in a large non-stick pan, add the onions and cook gently for 5 minutes until they soften. Stir in the Quorn and spices, then add the apricots and stock. Bring to the boil, then turn the heat down and cook gently for 10–15 minutes.
2 Meanwhile, make up the couscous according to the packet instructions – it will take about 450ml/16fl oz boiling water to give it a nice fluffy texture. Fork through the lemon zest and mint. Season to taste.
3 Spoon the couscous on to serving plates, pile the Quorn mixture on top and scatter with the cashews.

• Per serving 497 kcalories, protein 24g, carbohydrate 67g, fat 16g, saturated fat 2g, fibre 9g, added sugar none, salt 1.21g

Serve this bread and butter pudding, with its irresistible nut and cinnamon flavours, with a little single cream for pouring.

Raisin Bread and Butter Pudding

50g/2oz butter, softened, plus
extra for greasing
400g raisin loaf, crusts on
750ml/1¼ pints milk
142ml carton double cream
grated zest of 1 lemon
4 eggs
50g/2oz caster sugar
2 tbsp brandy or 1 tsp vanilla extract

FOR THE TOPPING
2 tbsp demerara sugar
2 tbsp chopped nuts
1 tsp ground cinnamon

Takes 1¼ hours–1 hour 20 minutes •
Serves 6

1 Butter a shallow 2 litre/3½ pint ovenproof dish. Spread each slice of raisin bread with the butter (don't use the end crusts). Halve the slices diagonally.

2 Put the milk, cream and lemon zest in a pan. Bring slowly to the boil, then cool so it's just lukewarm.

3 Beat the eggs and sugar. Add the brandy or vanilla and the warm lemon milk. Arrange half the bread over the base of the dish. Pour over half the milk mixture. Repeat the bread and milk layers. Let it soak for 15 minutes. Preheat the oven to 180°C/Gas 4/fan oven 160°C.

4 Mix the topping ingredients together. Sprinkle over the pudding. Bake for 40–45 minutes until golden brown and firm. Leave for 5 minutes before serving.

• Per serving 579 kcalories, protein 16g, carbohydrate 57g, fat 32g, saturated fat 15g, fibre none, added sugar 24g, salt 1.03g

The velvety texture of coconut cream makes a delicious ice cream and is invaluable for those on a no-dairy diet.

Pineapple and Coconut Ice

1 large and 1 medium golden pineapple
juice of 3 limes
175g/6oz golden icing sugar, sifted
200ml carton coconut cream

FOR THE SYRUP
100g/4oz golden caster sugar
1 cinnamon stick, split in pieces
mint leaves, to serve

Takes 40 minutes, plus freezing • Serves 6

1 Peel the large pineapple, cut it in half, then in quarters lengthways. Cut away core. Roughly chop the flesh, then whizz in a food processor to a rough purée. Tip into a bowl with the lime juice, icing sugar and coconut cream. Stir. Freeze for 2–3 hours until setting around the edges. Whisk to break up the large ice crystals, then freeze again until firm.
2 Meanwhile, peel, core and slice the other pineapple. Dissolve the sugar in 2 tablespoons of water in a pan. Add the cinnamon and boil until a syrup forms. Add the pineapple slices and poach for 2–3 minutes. Cool.
3 Transfer the ice cream to the fridge 30 minutes before serving. Serve with the poached pineapple and syrup, decorated with mint leaves and cinnamon from the poaching liquid.

• Per serving 397 kcalories, protein 2g, carbohydrate 75g, fat 12g, saturated fat 10g, fibre 3g, added sugar 48g, salt trace

An unusually light and fluffy cobbler makes an indulgent
pudding for Sunday lunch get-togethers.

Plum and Apple Cinnamon Cobbler

750g/1lb 10oz cooking apples
(Bramley's are best), peeled,
cored and stoned
juice of 1 lemon
100g/4oz golden caster sugar
350g/12oz ripe plums, halved,
stoned and quartered

FOR THE COBBLER
100g/4oz self-raising flour
1 tsp cinnamon
50g/2oz butter, cut into small pieces
50g/2oz golden caster sugar
1 egg, beaten
4 tbsp milk
50g/2oz walnut pieces

Takes 50 minutes–1 hour • Serves 4

1 Preheat the oven to 180°C/Gas 4/fan
oven 160°C. Butter a 1.5 litre/2¾ pint
ovenproof pie dish.
2 Put the apples in a pan with the lemon
juice, sugar and 1 tablespoon of water.
Bring to the boil, then cover and cook gently
for 5 minutes. Add the plums and cook for
a further 5 minutes.
3 Turn the fruit into the dish. Put the flour
and cinnamon in a bowl, add the butter and
rub in with your fingertips. Stir in the sugar.
Add the egg and milk and mix lightly to a soft
batter (this can be done in a food processor).
4 Drop tablespoonfuls of the batter over the
fruit, leaving gaps where the fruit peers
through. Scatter over the nuts. Bake for 25–30
minutes until the topping is crisp and brown.

• Per serving 556 kcalories, protein 8g, carbohydrate
90g, fat 21g, saturated fat 8g, fibre 6g, added sugar
37g, salt 0.3g

These muesli squares are really moist, chewy and packed with goodness – ideal for a snack or lunchbox.

Granola Bars

175g/6oz unsalted butter
140g/5oz clear honey
250g/9oz demerara sugar
350g/12oz porridge oats
1½ tsp ground cinnamon
85g/3oz shelled pecan nuts or walnuts
85g/3oz raisins
85g/3oz dried papaya or mango, chopped
85g/3oz dried apricots, chopped
85g/3oz pumpkin seeds
50g/2oz ground almonds
50g/2oz sesame seeds

Takes 35 minutes • Makes 9 squares

1 Preheat the oven to 190°C/Gas 5/fan oven 170°C. Line the base of a 23cm/9in square, 5cm/2in deep cake tin with greaseproof paper. Melt the butter and honey in a saucepan, then stir in the sugar.
2 Cook over a low heat for 5 minutes, stirring until the sugar has dissolved. Bring to the boil, then boil for 1–2 minutes, stirring, until thickened into a smooth caramel sauce.
3 Mix together all the remaining ingredients and stir into the sauce until well combined.
4 Spoon into the tin and press down with the back of a warm, wet spoon. Bake for 15 minutes until beginning to brown around the edges. Allow to cool a little. Run a sharp knife around the edge of the tin. Turn out, then peel off the lining paper. Cool, then cut into nine squares.

• Per square 696 kcalories, protein 11g, carbohydrate 85g, fat 37g, saturated fat 12g, fibre 6g, added sugar 41g, salt 0.06g

With an original flavour for an ice cream, this dessert
has an unusual but elegant taste.

Iced Ginger Cream

6 ready-made individual meringues
425ml carton double cream
grated zest of 1 lemon
3 tbsp kirsch
2 tbsp caster sugar
4 pieces of stem ginger in syrup,
finely chopped

Takes 20 minutes, plus chilling •
Serves 6

1 Line an 18cm/7in round sandwich cake tin with cling film. Break the meringues into chunks. Whisk the cream until just stiff, then fold in the lemon zest, kirsch, sugar, ginger and meringue pieces.
2 Spoon into the tin, level the top and put in the freezer for at least 4 hours.
3 Turn out of the tin 10 minutes before serving and chill. Cut into wedges and drizzle with the syrup from the jar of ginger.

• Per serving 333 kcalories, protein 2g, carbohydrate 22g, fat 26g, saturated fat 16g, fibre none, added sugar 19g, salt 0.54g

A healthy take on a favourite pudding – the muesli topping uses less fat and added sugar, so it's excellent for diabetics.

Apple and Ginger Crumble

800g/1lb 12oz Bramley's apples, peeled, cored and sliced
200ml/7fl oz unsweetened apple and mango pure fruit juice
1 piece stem ginger in syrup, finely chopped, plus 1 tbsp of syrup from the jar
reduced fat Greek yogurt or low-fat natural yogurt, to serve

FOR THE TOPPING
100g/4oz plain wholemeal flour
85g/3oz olive oil spread (59% vegetable fat), chilled
100g/4oz wholewheat muesli with no added salt or sugar
3 tbsp light muscovado sugar
25g/1oz sunflower seeds

Takes 1–1½ hours • Serves 5–6

1 Preheat the oven to 190°C/Gas 5/fan oven 170°C. Put the apples in a 1.5 litre/ 2¾ pint pie dish. Pour over the fruit juice, then add the ginger and 1 tablespoon of the syrup and stir together.
2 To make the topping, tip the flour into a large bowl. Add the olive oil spread and cut into small pieces using a round-bladed knife, so that it is evenly distributed through the flour. Stir in the muesli, sugar and sunflower seeds, then scatter evenly over the apples to cover them.
3 Bake for 40–45 minutes until golden and crunchy on top. Leave to cool slightly for 5–10 minutes before serving with reduced fat Greek yogurt or low-fat natural yogurt.

• Per serving 380 kcalories, protein 6g, carbohydrate 58g, fat 15g, saturated fat 3g, fibre 6g, added sugar 11g, salt 0.46g

Stem ginger is a classic combination with melon,
but it's lovely with strawberries, too.

Strawberry, Melon and Ginger Puds

½ medium cantaloupe melon (about 350g/12oz), skinned, seeded and cut into chunks
250g/9oz strawberries, hulled and sliced
4 ginger biscuits, roughly crushed
2 pieces of stem ginger in syrup (about 25g/1oz), chopped, plus 2 tbsp of syrup from the jar
2 × 150g pots 0% Greek yogurt
4 tsp light muscovado sugar

Takes 15–25 minutes • Serves 4

1 Gently mix the melon and strawberries together in a large bowl, then pile half the fruit into four glass tumblers. Sprinkle with half the biscuit crumbs.
2 Stir the chopped ginger and syrup into the yogurt and spoon into the tumblers. Pile the rest of the fruit on top, then scatter with the remaining biscuit crumbs.
3 Sprinkle a teaspoon of muscovado sugar on top of each dessert and chill until ready to serve (you can make this up to 2 hours ahead). The sugar will gradually melt to give a yummy toffee flavour.
4 Take the tumblers out of the fridge about 15 minutes before serving, so they are not too chilled.

• Per serving 168 kcalories, protein 8.9g, carbohydrate 30g, fat 2.2g, saturated fat 0.6g, fibre 1.5g, added sugar 10.3g, salt 0.4g

Based on the Baked Alaska idea – baked ice cream
and meringue – but using a moist ginger cake.

Baked Ginger Pudding

227g can pineapple chunks in
natural juice
1 ready-made Jamaica ginger cake,
sliced horizontally
3 egg whites
175g/6oz light muscovado sugar
500ml carton vanilla ice cream

Takes 20 minutes • Serves 4

1 Preheat the oven to 220°C/Gas 7/fan oven 200°C. Drain the pineapple, reserving 3 tablespoons of juice. Put the ginger cake slices side by side in a rectangular shallow ovenproof dish. Drizzle over the pineapple juice and pineapple chunks.

2 Whisk the egg whites until stiff. Whisk in the sugar, a tablespoon at a time, whisking well between each addition until the meringue is thick and glossy.

3 Slice the ice cream and cover the fruit and sponge with it, pressing down to level. Completely cover with the meringue, swirling the top with a fork. Bake for 5 minutes until golden. Serve at once.

• Per serving 484 kcalories, protein 9g, carbohydrate 85g, fat 14g, saturated fat 7g, fibre 1g, added sugar 59g, salt 0.53g

Perfect with a cup of tea at home or for an afternoon summer picnic. And they'll keep for up to 5 days in a plastic container in the fridge.

Apricot Crumb Squares

175g/6oz plain flour
140g/5oz light muscovado sugar
140g/5oz butter, softened
1 tsp ground cinnamon
icing sugar, for dusting

FOR THE CAKE
175g/6oz butter, softened
200g/8oz golden caster sugar
3 large eggs
175g/6oz plain flour
1 tsp baking powder
2–3 tbsp milk
8 fresh apricots, quartered (or canned in natural juice)

Takes about 1¼ hours •
Makes 16 squares

1 Preheat the oven to 180°C/Gas 4/fan oven 160°C. Butter a shallow 22cm/8½in square cake tin. Put the flour, muscovado sugar, butter and cinnamon in a food processor with ½ teaspoon of salt and blend to make a sticky crumble.

2 Using an electric hand whisk or wooden spoon, blend the cake ingredients, except the milk and apricots. Gradually add enough milk to make a creamy mixture that drops from the spoon. Spread in the tin and scatter with apricots. Top with the crumble and press down.

3 Bake for 45–50 minutes until golden and a skewer comes out clean. Cool in the tin, then cut into 16 squares and dust with icing sugar.

• Per square 332 kcalories, protein 4g, carbohydrate 42g, fat 18g, saturated fat 11g, fibre 1g, added sugar 22g, salt 0.52g

Not only a great and popular finish to a Sunday lunch,
this is also a brilliant way to cook rhubarb.

Rhubarb Streusel Pie

500g pack shortcrust pastry, thawed
if frozen
1kg/2lb 4oz rhubarb, trimmed, or
750g/1lb 10oz ready trimmed
3 rounded tbsp plain flour
85g/3oz caster sugar
single cream or vanilla ice cream,
to serve

FOR THE TOPPING
85g/3oz plain flour
1 tsp ground cinnamon
50g/2oz demerara sugar
50g/2oz hazelnuts, roughly chopped
50g/2oz butter, cut into small pieces

Takes 1 hour–1¼ hours • Serves 6–8

1 Roll out the pastry and use to line a deep 23cm/9in flan tin. Chop the rhubarb into 3cm/1in lengths and tip into a large bowl with the flour and sugar. Mix well, then tip into the pastry case, spreading the rhubarb to level it.
2 To make the topping, mix together the flour, cinnamon, sugar and nuts. Add the butter and rub in with your fingertips until the mixture resembles coarse breadcrumbs. Sprinkle evenly over the top of the rhubarb. Set aside for up to 6 hours, until ready to bake.
3 Preheat the oven to 190°C/Gas 5/fan oven 170°C. Bake the pie for 40–45 minutes until the topping is crisp and golden and the rhubarb is tender – test by spearing a piece of fruit through the topping with a knife. Serve warm or cold with single cream or vanilla ice cream.

• Per serving for six 665 kcalories, protein 8g, carbohydrate 81g, fat 36g, saturated fat 15g, fibre 5g, added sugar 24g, salt 0.51g

You can find small bottles of blackcurrant coulis in supermarket chiller cabinets alongside the creams, or by the canned fruit.

Apple Flapjack Trifle

100g/4oz porridge oats
1 tsp mixed spice
50g/2oz light muscovado sugar
50g/2oz butter

FOR THE FILLING
7–8 Coxes or russet apples, depending on size
25g/1oz butter
25g/1oz golden caster sugar
2 tablespoons blackcurrant coulis
500g carton fresh custard
284ml carton double cream

Takes 25–30 minutes, plus cooling • Serves 6

1 Mix the oats, spice and sugar. Melt the butter in a frying pan, add the oat mixture and fry for about 5 minutes, stirring all the time, until it is lightly toasted and crisp. Tip into a bowl and leave to cool.

2 Peel, core and thickly slice the apples. Melt the butter for the filling in the frying pan until it is foaming. Add the apples, fry over a high heat and turn them as they colour. Sprinkle over the sugar and cook for a further 2–3 minutes, until the apples are slightly softened. Leave to cool.

3 Layer half the apples and almost half the oats in a glass serving dish. Repeat, setting aside a few oats. Drizzle over the coulis, then spoon over the custard. Whip the cream until stiff, then spoon over the custard. Scatter over the reserved oat mixture and serve.

• Per serving 573 kcalories, protein 6g, carbohydrate 54g, fat 38g, saturated fat 23g, fibre 3g, added sugar 21g, salt 0.3g

Index

215   Index

Picture credits and recipe credits

BBC Worldwide would like to thank the following for providing photographs. While very effort has been made to trace and acknowledge all photographers, we would like to apologize should there be any errors or omissions.

Marie-Louise Avery p17, p23, p35, p39, p117, p121; Iain Bagwell p105, p125, p157, p175; Steve Baxter p27, p65, p152, p207; Martin Brigdale p131; Ken Field p15, p83; David Munns p25, p45, p49, p97, p113, p165, p193, p197, p199; Myles New p59, p61, p63, p87, p201; Michael Paul p29; Craig Robertson p41, p99, p119, p133, p147; Howard Shooter p33, p43, p53, p137, p155, p163, p183, p203; Roger Stowell p11, p13, p19, p21, p37, p47, p51, p57, p67, p69, p71, p73, p75, p77, p81, p85, p89, p91, p93, p101, p103, p107, p109, p111, p115, p123, p127, p129, p135, p141, p143, p145, p149, p151, p161, p167, p169, p171, p173, p177, p179, p185, p187, p189, p191, p205; Simon Walton p55, p79. p159, p181; Simon Wheeler p95, p139, p195, p211; Geoff Wilkinson p31, p209

All the recipes in this book have been created by the editorial team on *BBC Good Food Magazine*:
Sue Ashworth, Lorna Brash, Sara Buenfeld, Mary Cadogan, Barney Desmazery, Kate Moseley, Vicky Musselman, Angela Nilsen, Maggie Pannell, Thane Prince, Jenny White, Jeni Wright